A Look at Life *from the* Riverbank

Steve Chapman

HARVEST HOUSE PUBLISHERS
EUGENE, OREGON

Contents

A Note from Steve

The outdoors is one of the best places to discover more about God! "Since the creation of the world God's invisible qualities—his eternal power and divine nature—have been clearly seen, being understood from what has been made." These inspiring words from Romans 1:20 (NIV) reveal the undeniable truth that casting a line while sitting on the banks of a river or lake, floating in a canoe, or trolling in a boat gives us incredible opportunities to contemplate God's creation and how we can develop into the people He created us to be. If we take the time to "get out there," God will make Himself known—and often in ways we never expect.

If you relish having rod and reel in hand and enjoy swapping stories, *A Look at Life from the Riverbank* is for you! As you join me on some fun and exciting fishing trips, you'll also, hopefully, glean some wisdom based on God's Word that will help you better navigate the river called life.

1

Ready to Fish!

You will seek the LORD your God, and you will find Him if
you search for Him with all your heart and all your soul.

DEUTERONOMY 4:29

Jack Adams greeted his sister and her family after they pulled their minivan into the driveway at his new house in the country. His nephew Billy quickly swung the back door open, jumped out, and ran to the rear of the vehicle. Within less than a minute the 12-year-old had everything he needed in hand to do what he'd dreamed about during the 300-mile ride to his uncle's farm. He was ready to fish at the huge pond he'd only seen in pictures.

With excitement he finally turned to his uncle. "Great to see you, Uncle Jack! Do you mind if I go fishing in your pond?"

Uncle Jack smiled and put his hand out for a shake.

Billy set his tackle box on the ground and shook his uncle's hand.

"You bet you can fish in that pond, young man!" Billy's understanding uncle replied. "I hope your arm muscles are in shape 'cause there are some brutes in there that will test your steel." He smiled broadly as he pointed the way to the water.

Billy's eyes widened at his uncle's report. He quickly turned to head toward the pond. After just one step, though, he stopped and looked back. "Where's the best place to catch 'em, Uncle Jack?"

"In the water, Billy!" Jack laughed when Billy's rolling eyes signaled that he'd gotten the joke. Then the older man gave his young nephew some advice that had a biblical ring to it. "If you seek 'em, you'll find 'em, Billy. Just don't give up. They're there for the findin'!"

The strength of desire Billy had for fishing is a great illustration of how strong the yearning is in humans to look for some kind of meaning in life. And what Billy did for his quest for fish is similar to what we do to find God.

- *Billy didn't deny his desire to go fishing.* Instead, he gladly embraced it and let it permeate every cell of his being. He couldn't wait to get to his uncle's farm! Embracing our longing for God is the first step in finding Him.

- *Billy set his mind on wetting a line.* When he got to his uncle's farm, his heart and mind had been consumed by fishing for 300 miles. If our thoughts are saturated with finding God on our journey through life, we will.

- *Billy's yearning for catching fish reached into his spirit.* The depth of his yearning pushed him onward to the pond. If our longing to find God goes as deep, it is inevitable that we'll experience the great joy of feeling the tug of His presence in our lives.

May your search for your Creator and His guidance be just as exciting as Billy's quest for fish! If it is, you'll find your Lord and Savior—after all, He's there for the findin'!

God, I'm thankful You put the desire in me to seek You out. I'm glad You helped me find You. I need You. I want to reconnect with You. In Christ's name I pray, amen.

2

Crossing the Creek

God carried you, just as a man carries his son.

DEUTERONOMY 1:31

Sam and his eight-year-old son, Shawn, had caught a few blue-gill and a couple of small catfish out of the creek they were fishing. Hoping for something bigger in size, they slowly worked their way upstream on the brushy bank. When they came to a rocky cliff on their side of the stream they could go no farther. That's when Sam saw it.

"Look up there past this rock, Shawn. There's the hole we need to be fishing in!"

Because Shawn wasn't as knowledgeable as his dad about what made the pool look so good, he asked, "Why there, Dad?"

"'Cause it looks deep and like the kind of place the bigger fish would favor. We need to give it a try, but we have a problem."

"What's that, Dad?"

Sam sighed deep. "We can't get there from here. We have to cross to the other side."

Shawn looked at the brisk flow of water and challenged his dad about going across. "Dad, I don't think I'm tall enough to get through the creek. I'm not sure I want to try it."

Sam answered his son with confidence, "I'll just carry you across, Sam. You can get on my shoulders and hold our rods and reels and the tackle box. We'll make it just fine."

Sam swallowed hard. "If you think you can do it without drowning us, I'll go along."

"Trust me, little buddy. We'll be fine."

Sam wasn't fully convinced, but he made the climb onto his dad's wide shoulders. Holding the tackle box with one hand and their two rods in the other, he squeezed his legs tightly around his dad's neck, nearly choking him in an effort to hold steady.

Sam stepped into the cool water and slowly made his way through the current. At the deepest part, the water level reached just above his belt and occasionally splashed the bottoms of Shawn's boots.

"We're gonna make it, son. Just keep your balance and look straight ahead!" Sam said.

Two minutes later the father and son stood safely on the opposite side of the creek. As Shawn dismounted from his dad's shoulders, he grinned big and thanked his dad for delivering him safely across the stream. Within two minutes they both were throwing baited hooks into the deep pool.

Sam carrying his son across the creek reminds me of the illustration found in today's verse. The statement "God carried you, just as a man carries his son" was made to help the Israelites remember that the God who had delivered them through the wilderness was the same God who would go before them to help them defeat the giants that occupied the land He'd instructed them to claim.

Even with the memory of God's amazing deliverance, the Israelites still didn't trust Him. Personally, I don't want to be guilty of such a thing. To discount those times in my past when God carried me on His shoulders like Sam carried Shawn wouldn't be a wise thing to do. I'm sure you too are determined to avoid that mistake. May God help us to always let the memory of past deliverances contribute to our confidence for future victories.

Thank You, heavenly Father, for all those times You carried me safely through dangerous waters. Help me never forget the safety of Your shoulders. Remind me to always be willing to climb on them when I need to get to the other side of life's challenging waters. In Your Son's name I pray, amen.

3

Water Grave

*We have been buried with [Jesus] through
baptism into death, so that as Christ was raised
from the dead through the glory of the Father,
so we too might walk in newness of life.*

ROMANS 6:4

The concrete boat ramp that led down to the Ohio River provided convenient access to a good fishing spot during my younger years. To the left of the pavement, about 40 yards down, was a big, brown-colored rock that slightly jutted out over the water. Climbing up on it provided an excellent, obstruction-free casting place. The rock was also a clear observation point to watch the activity at the ramp.

Some of it was quite entertaining, like the day a fellow backed his empty trailer into the water, got out of his truck to load his motorboat, and realized the pickup's brakes weren't working. He managed to get back in and rescue his four-wheel friend as the water reached the floorboards. What was especially memorable was the way the man screamed the moment his rig started rolling backward. His voice held the distinct tone of impending financial doom.

On another day, while waiting for a river resident to take the shrimp on my hook, I looked over at the ramp. It was empty, so I recalled what had happened there about three years earlier. Several members of the congregation that my dad pastored left the Sunday morning service and made their way to this place at the water's edge. It was baptism day for a half-dozen candidates. I was one of two teens among that group. We were dressed in older clothes and ready for our immersion.

The icy, March waters of the Ohio stinging my legs as I waded in is something I won't ever forget. My dad was doing the "dunking honors" that day, and though I was sitting on the rock nearly three years later, in my mind I could still hear his voice loud and clear as he announced, "In the name of the Father, the Son, and the Holy Ghost, I baptize Steve today!"

When I went under water, the chill was incredibly intense, but at the same time there was a strange warming comfort that came over me. I felt invigorated! I smiled as I waded all the way back to the ramp and enjoyed the relief that came with the thick blanket my mother threw over my shoulders. As I continued to fish and think about my baptism experience, I recalled how Dad explained the meaning of it to us.

"Today you are demonstrating outwardly what has taken place inwardly. You are testifying with the apostle Paul, who wrote to the Galatian believers, 'I have been crucified with Christ; and it is no longer I who live, but Christ lives in me.' And because you have died with Christ, it is time to be buried with Him in the waters of baptism. As you rise from the water, you'll be declaring that you have also risen with Jesus Christ from your spiritual death that was caused by sin. This is a day of rejoicing for you!"

These many years later the rock where I fished is gone, but the concrete boat ramp is still there. I've gone back to it from time to time to remember my spiritual "death, burial, and resurrection." While standing at the water's edge remembering the experience, a song lyric was born about baptism. Dogwood, the band I was in when I wrote it, recorded it, and eventually other artists recorded it as well. Amazingly, it can still be heard on the web! One of my favorite renderings is by the group known as The Imperials. If you want to hear it, go online and simply type in "Water Grave Imperials," in the search engine window and their version should come up. If you've been baptized, listen to the song and rejoice with the memory. If not, you'll better understand what it means to go down to your "water grave." [If you want to listen to Dogwood's version (recorded at the Koinonia Family Reunion, 2007), type in "watergrave dogwood."]

Father, thank You for Your Son, Jesus, who died for me, was buried for me, and was resurrected for me. I accept His completed work on my behalf. I'm thankful You asked me to demonstrate my decision to embrace what He's done in my heart by being baptized. What a uniquely beautiful way to testify that Jesus was crucified for my sins, was buried, and then was raised from the dead, just as I too am raised to newness of life through Him. Heavenly Father, I praise Your holy name for this marvelous and eternal gift. In Your Son's name I pray, amen.

4

Just Add Water

*These words, which I am commanding you
today...[you] shall talk of them when you sit in
your house and when you walk by the way and
when you lie down and when you rise up.*

DEUTERONOMY 6:6-7

Today's familiar verse seems custom written for busy parents. I'm not sure how moms and dads did it in times past, but in our time in history our "wall to wall" lives, especially for those with multiple kids, can drain both brain and brawn. With our jobs and responsibilities and the countless activities for our kids, including school, sports, music lessons, dance lessons, and trips to friends' houses (to name just a few), the result is obvious—no time to make time for really connecting with our kids.

A "90-miles-per-hour lifestyle" makes today's Deuteronomy 6 verses even more important for parents, especially dads. Why? Because it includes an option that a lot of guys prefer—"when you walk by the way." Unlike lots of moms who are very fine with sitting at home or at a bedside talking with their children, many dads would rather take the communication thing outside where they can "*do* and talk."

There are as many things a dad can do with a kid in the outdoors as there are dads and kids to do them. Some prefer throwing a ball, some like the exciting action of riding a bicycle, while others would rather leisurely stroll down a long fairway. While the choices are vast, one thing remains constant: The movement of a man's arms and legs can be the gears that make his tongue work. For me, fishing with my kids did the trick.

If you're not familiar with how fishing can oil the gears of conversation, here's a brief explanation…

Going fishing requires driving or walking to the water, which means you're side by side with your kid(s). While fishing, it's likely that you're shoulder to shoulder or within easy earshot of each other. Add to that the constant motion that comes with casting, baiting hooks, dodging flying hooks, eating, baiting, de-hooking (hopefully from the fish's mouth and not from an earlobe), tying knots, and eating some more, and a guy's mouth seems to move more easily.

What's particularly amazing about how action can activate male conversation is that sometimes the words said are from deeper places in the heart than expected. While a bluegill is tugging on a line, rarely heard words such as *I love you, I'm proud of you*, and *I'm so glad you're mine* can flow out and touch a tender place in a child's heart. For some, these spoken words can literally change their lives forever.

How great of God to provide us dads with the practicality of action to help us talk and also provide a place like a fishing spot for it to happen. He's made being a dad a lot less complicated. All we dads need is the right ingredients and then add water.

Just Add Water

If you want to make a sweet memory with your kids,
    here's the recipe
Peanut butter and a jar of jam, a loaf of bread,
    and pop in a can
Bamboo poles and hooks on the line, a can of worms,
    and some of your time
And don't forget that little round bobber—
    then all you do is just add water

Just add water, don't have to be deep
Take 'em to the banks of a big lake or a little creek
Sweet memories with your sons and your daughters
That's what you'll get when you just add water

You can take your phone but leave it off,
    turn on your heart and let it talk
'Cause words come easy when you're fishing,
    and when they talk make sure you listen
If the weather turns hot and the fish go hide,
    don't pack it up and run back inside
Tell the kids, "Do like your father!" then roll up your
    pants and just add water.

Father in heaven, thank You for how practical and easy You've made it to be a dad who talks with my kids. Thank You for the tools You've given to help me be better with my words—especially water and fish! In Christ's name I pray, amen.

5

Fish Tacos?

The greatest among you will be your servant.

MATTHEW 23:11 NIV

The first time I heard the words *fish* and *taco* used together, I was at an eatery on the Gulf of Mexico coast with some friends. We sat down and opened the menu and there it was! Listed right there with grilled salmon, blackened trout, and several other "normal" dishes. When I muttered the combination of words *fish taco*, quite honestly I almost gagged. I felt like all my taste buds ran to the back of my throat and jumped down it. I looked across the table and said to the person who had chosen the restaurant. "Are they kidding about *fish tacos?*"

Everyone at the table laughed except me. Why? They were from the coast! To them the words made perfect sense together. So not wanting to appear to be an uncultured wimp, I braved up and ordered my first fish tacos. I've never been the same since. I'm now in serious like with a flour tortilla folded in half and filled with lettuce, tomato, special sauce, and a generous serving of fresh fried cod, or snapper, or whatever is available from the marine world (except squid). The fact is, I may well be the number one fan these days of fish tacos on the entire planet.

In my mind (and on my palette), *fish taco* is a great example of an oxymoron. The term is sort of like an "authentic replica," or "alone together," or "controlled chaos." Phrases like these can mess with my head on first hearing, but with some thought and time, after a while they can make sense.

The Bible has some word combinations that can be classified as oxymorons too. Today's verse from Matthew 23 is a very good example. On first reading, a new believer might say, "Is God serious about this? If a person is going to be great he or she has to be a servant? Where's the sense in that?"

The reason such a statement is hard to process in a mind new to the Bible is that very often his or her idea of greatness isn't the same as God's idea. In this world the people considered great are those who are served by other people. In God's kingdom, where things are *really* different (even opposite), those who are great are those who serve. Why? Because when a person serves, he or she is mirroring the life of Christ who "did not come to be served but to serve, and to give His life a ransom for many" (Matthew 20:28).

Another example of a biblical oxymoron is found in Matthew 20:16: "So the last shall be first, and the first last." Again, in this world the one who comes across the line first is considered the winner, but in God's kingdom the winners are the people who graciously allow others to cross the line ahead of them. This is not a mind-set that will advance a career necessarily, but it is a way of thinking that pleases God. And pleasing God is the greatest of all accomplishments. Here are a few other notable oxymoron moments in the Scriptures.

- "Whoever wishes to save his life will lose it; but whoever loses his life for My sake will find it" (Matthew 16:25).
- "When I am weak, then I am strong" (2 Corinthians 12:10).
- "The foolishness of God is wiser than men, and the weakness of God is stronger than men" (1 Corinthians 1:25).
- "Though your sins are as scarlet, they will be as white as snow" (Isaiah 1:18). (This is one of my favorites!)

I hope you'll take the time to meditate on these incredibly insightful verses. If you do, I suspect you'll find the truths in them can literally and eternally change your life. Perhaps you can think about them while enjoying some fish tacos.

Lord, how true that Your ways are not my ways, that Your thoughts are not my thoughts, and that You see things quite differently than I do. Help me to always be accepting of this truth. Thank You for the many times in Your written Word that You help me see it. In Christ's name I pray, amen.

6

Salt-Seasoned Bait

*Let your speech always be with grace, as though
seasoned with salt, so that you will know how
you should respond to each person.*

COLOSSIANS 4:6

As a member of an organization in Nashville that assists songwriters in honing their skills, I attended a workshop conducted by an expert in the field. Among the many useful tips he gave to those of us passionate about creating lyrics and music, one suggestion especially caught my ear. As a setup for the unforgettable tip, he first reminded us that the "hook" of a song is a repeated phrase specifically designed to catch the ear of the listener. With that in mind, he *challenged* us to seriously consider what we're putting on the hook. He said, "If you go fishing, you wouldn't bait the hook for yourself. You bait it for the fish. For that reason. it's important that you know the food preference of the fish and the best possible way to present it."

The teacher went on to say it is always a wonderful accomplishment for a songwriter to create something that he or she really likes. However, if that's the only goal the writer has, he or she risks having a song that may fall short of having a broad appeal to listeners. He told us, and this is my paraphrase, "Folks, your self-satisfying song might make you feel good while you're singing it, but don't be surprised if the audience, or worse, a potential publisher, returns an uninterested stare as they hear it."

Since that workshop, I've kept the "write to the fish, not the fisherman" songwriting wisdom in mind. It resulted in a useful and advantageous adjustment to my writing process. But songwriting isn't the only area of my life his sage advice affected. These days I also consider what I'm putting on my hook when it comes to all forms of communication. I want the words I say when I'm not holding a guitar to be more enticing and appealing too. I want to point people to Jesus in everything I do!

If offering words to others that are more pleasing is your goal like it is mine, today's verse offers great advice for us to follow. Basically, Paul admonished *every* believer, not just the believers in Colossi, to let their speech be "salted" with grace when talking to outsiders or nonbelievers. Why? Conversation seasoned with salt is an effective way to create thirst in listeners. When they're thirsty, they'll want to hear more. Paul is telling you and me to put "salt-seasoned bait" on our hooks!

The question then is "What is 'salt-seasoned speech'?" One good way to answer the question is to consider at least three things it *is not*:

- *Salt-seasoned speech is not wishy-washy.* Matthew 5:37 instructs us to let our statements be yes or no because "anything beyond is of evil." While this verse is about making oaths, it also applies to all areas of our speech, including how we share our faith. Talking to someone about Christ while displaying a confident and unwavering belief in Him is far more appealing and convincing than talking about Him with a tone of reservation. Hesitation may damage the hearer's willingness to accept the truth of the gospel. We don't want to be wishy-washy about our own belief in Jesus.

- *Salt-seasoned speech is not corrupted with unwholesomeness.* Ephesians 4:29 has the best advice regarding the cleanliness of our speech: "Let no unwholesome word proceed from your mouth." The word *unwholesome* means "rotten" or "diseased," like fruit that has gone really bad. What could be more unattractive to an unbeliever than hearing a person who claims to follow Christ use language that sounds putrid?

- *Salt-seasoned speech is not laced with obscenity.* Ephesians
  5:3-4 says it plainly: "Immorality or any impurity or greed
  must not even be named among you…There must be no
  filthiness and silly talk, or coarse jesting, which are not fitting, but rather giving of thanks."

So what *is* salt-seasoned speech? Once again, the Bible offers the
best answer. It is found in the last part of Ephesians 4:29. "Let no
unwholesome word proceed from your mouth…only such a word as
is good for edification according to the need of the moment, so that *it
will give grace to those who hear.*" To *edify* is to "build another person up,
especially in an area they might need encouragement."

Proverbs 25 contains the best bait for our "hook of conversation":
"A word fitly spoken is like apples of gold in a setting of silver" (verse
11 ESV). There is not a fish in the world that wouldn't go for such tasty
morsels.

*Father, I am grateful for every opportunity You provide to share
You with others. Help me always be mindful of the kind of bait
I put on my "hook of conversation." May my words always be
gracious and attractive to the ears of those who hear. I want to
honor You in everything I say and do. In Christ's name I pray,
amen.*

7

Be Careful!

Watch yourself, that you do not forget the LORD.

DEUTERONOMY 6:12

There's hardly anything better tasting in the fish department than fresh-caught, well-seasoned, microwaved cobia (lemon fish)... and lots of it. My son and daughter and I, along with two friends, learned this firsthand while on an overnight trip fishing in the Gulf of Mexico.

We were aboard a chartered boat in the deep waters of the Gulf. Our trip had yielded a full day of arm-tiring, back-straining reeling in of our limit of heavy lemon fish. When dinnertime came, we were hungry enough to eat the rods and reels. Our host captain saw the famished looks on our faces and chose a plump 25-pounder lemon to cut up into two-inch-thick steaks for dinner.

With plenty of ketchup and tartar sauce to dip the fish in, we tore into the feast like a school of piranha. Elbows and fingers were flying as we dug in, smacked our lips, and handed our plates to the captain for refills. I refer to such a culinary experience as a "gastronomical jubilee."

Within a half-hour, the kids, my two friends, and I were sitting on the deck rubbing our bellies and smiling under the dimming light of the colorful evening sky. The temperature was a perfect 72, and gentle waves tenderly rocked the boat. Like babies drifting off to sleep after a full bottle, all of us allowed our eyes to droop and then close as if sealing in the satisfaction we felt in our tummies.

After a few minutes of blissful dozing, I woke up and looked around at my kids and our friends. The nearly comatose state we were in following the meal was rather comical. We were sprawled out on the benches in the boat like a bunch of lifeless octopuses. Arms and legs seemed to go in all directions. The bottom line is that we were worthless when it came to even thinking about doing something productive.

As I sat there looking through my sleepy, half-opened eyes, I noticed our energetic captain hurling baited hooks into the water and then placing the heavy-duty rods in the trolling cradles at the back of the boat. He was getting ready to night fish for shark. Before he could complete the process with all the rods, one of the poles danced wildly.

He barked out an order: "Somebody come and grab this rod! Let's catch a shark!"

Nobody moved. We didn't even want to. We couldn't! We were so full of delicious lemons (and all the tasty accoutrements) that we were like useless slugs. I was very glad we weren't on a vessel of war and that none of us had been called to man a cannon. I'm sure we'd have all gone down with the ship if that had been the case. As much as we loved fishing, it seemed we'd forgotten that fishing was why we were on the boat. The tighter our stomachs got, the looser our grip became on the purpose for the trip.

In thinking back to that wonderful trip, Deuteronomy 6:10-11 comes to mind. It addresses a similar situation with a far more serious result for God's people. The Israelites were entering into the land God had given them to possess:

> Then it shall come about when the LORD your God brings you into the land which He swore to your fathers, Abraham, Isaac and Jacob, to give you, great and splendid cities which you did not build, and houses full of all good things which you did not fill, and hewn cisterns which you did not dig, vineyards and olive trees which you did not plant, and you eat and are satisfied, then watch yourself, that you do not forget the LORD who brought you from the land of Egypt, out of the house of slavery.

After our onboard buffet experience, I better understand why God gave His people such a sobering warning. My kids, our friends, and I were riding in a boat we didn't build, using rods and reels we didn't buy, eating a meal we didn't prepare, floating on water we didn't form, catching fish we didn't create, using hooks we didn't bait. With all that pampering, it's no wonder we allowed the delicious, massive meal to knock us out. In our satisfied stupor, we couldn't remember how much we loved fishing!

When it comes to *not* making the mistake of forgetting how much we love and appreciate God's goodness to us, we need to be on the alert lest we allow all His blessings to lull us into a careless slumber. Just like God gave a heads-up to His people about this error *before* they went in to possess the promised land, He says to all of us who follow Him today and who enjoy His many blessings, "Watch yourself!"

God, I thank You for the countless blessings You've lavished on me. As wonderful as they are, I don't want to ever let them hinder my remembrance that You are the one who provides and that You alone delivered me through the wilderness of sin so I can enter into the joy of Your eternal presence. Thank You! In Christ's name I pray, amen.

8

The Unseen Presence

*You heard the sound of words, but you
saw no form—only a voice.*

DEUTERONOMY 4:12

I'll never forget how exciting it was when my first king salmon latched onto the artificial lure that trolled through the waters of Lake Michigan just off the coast of Muskegon, Michigan. There were five of us standing around when the deckhand yelled, "Who's first?" We all looked at each other, essentially asking, "Is it me?"

Finally Beau, the youngest among us, got the nod from all the adults, and he gladly engaged in the opening fight. Several minutes later we were all smiling as an 18-pound king flopped at our feet. The brute reluctantly took its place in the live well and became the first of nearly 40 big ones we landed over two days.

Throughout the morning, we each took turns doing battle with kings and lake trout, while the others took photographs documenting the fun. Around nine o'clock, a welcome lull in the action gave our arms a rest. With coffee cups steaming we shared the first versions of the stories we'd tell everyone when we got back to our home states.

Suddenly one of the rod tips bent over sharply as if bowing to royalty. Everyone knew that whatever had chomped down on the lure and ran with it was no small specimen. Responding to the deckhand's excited instructions, we scrambled to make room for whoever was brave enough to take on the challenge of matching muscles with it. I could see that the Alabaman among us had that unmistakable gleam in his eye that silently begged, *Please, let it be me!*

"It's Chuck's turn," I said, although it took everything within me to beat down my own desire and give way to his.

Chuck grinned and grunted as he fought the hard-running beast. The sound of unwinding line filled the air.

We could hardly wait to feast our eyes on whatever behemoth he was going to bring up. Several minutes passed while we rubbernecked the surrounding waters watching for a flash of silver. I didn't take my eyes off the surface as I readied my video camera to document the catch.

Suddenly, the tip of the rod straightened. The line that had been super tight a moment before dangled loosely over the stern. The big one had gotten away.

Chuck was instantly baptized in a pool of disappointment. Knowing that a broken line spelled defeat, he lowered his head for a few seconds and then headed for the cooler filled with soft drinks and juice. No one said a word. We simply allowed the letdown to run its path. Chuck sipped on a can of orange juice and looked out across the water. His jaw muscles throbbed with frustration for not having landed the trophy.

I quietly watched the man deal with the emotion that comes with such a defeat. As I wondered what was going through his mind, I decided I had to ask. "Bet that hurts, huh?"

"Yep. Sure does."

My friend didn't get to see the great king. He only heard the strength of its voice in the scream of the unwinding reel. Though he was downcast, the smile returned to his face 15 minutes later when his name was called again to manhandle a bent-over rod.

A few weeks later I thought of Chuck when I was reading Deuteronomy 4:15-20. In this passage Moses recounts the experience God's people had when they'd been at Horeb (Mt. Sinai):

> You came near and stood at the foot of the mountain, and the mountain burned with fire to the very heart of the heavens: darkness, cloud and thick gloom. Then the LORD spoke to you from the midst of the fire; you heard the

sound of words, but you saw no form—only a voice (Deuteronomy 4:11-13).

The Israelites only heard God speak. They couldn't see Him. Chuck could only gauge the size of his fish by the whine of the reel letting line out. He couldn't actually see the salmon. The difference between the Israelites at Mount Sinai and my friend on Lake Michigan was that although Chuck would have loved to see the huge fish, after a few minutes of adjustment, he seemed satisfied with just knowing it was there. The Israelites, however, weren't content to just hear God. They wanted to see Him or make a representative of Him they could see. As a result, they unwisely chose to make a molten image of a calf to worship (Exodus 32:1-5).

If the Israelites thought they were honoring the unseen God by bowing down before an object they could see, they were dangerously wrong. God didn't take kindly to an idol taking His place. Moses was well aware that the people were prone to engage in idol worship, and for that reason he was warning them about making the same mistake: "Since you did not see any form on the day the LORD spoke to you at Horeb...do not act corruptly and make a graven image for yourselves in the form of any figure" (Deuteronomy 4:15).

My friend, God hasn't changed. He still isn't pleased when His people choose to worship something seen over His yet-to-be-seen majesty. Unfortunately, far too many people are guilty of making such an error. Whether it's gold or silver, what they can buy, or any other temporal thing, making an idol of it to worship or to represent the God who provided it is not pleasing to God.

The day will come when our eyes will actually behold Him! Until then, may we be satisfied with hearing His voice through His written Word, the Bible. Through it we know He is real and He is great. Jesus said, "Blessed are they who did not see, and yet believed" (John 20:29).

Thank You, God, for the mystery of Your presence. Surely Your form is even greater than my finite mind can imagine. Until the day I see You, I will remain joyful and faithful by hearing Your voice through Your holy Word and prayer. In Christ's name I pray, amen.

9

Fish Heads and Sin

You shall utterly destroy them.

DEUTERONOMY 7:2

Charlie couldn't fight the urge to get one last fishing trip in before he and his family headed north to visit his in-laws for several days. It was springtime, and he was sure the crappie would be practically floating in line to bite whatever bait he dropped into the lake. The morning on the water was exactly like he'd imagined. The wind was calm, the temperature perfect, and there was plenty of line tugging to enjoy. Smiling and satisfied to have a dozen, good-sized fish on his stringer, Charlie trailered his small boat and returned to the house in plenty of time to clean the fish and get ready for their midafternoon departure.

Normally, the fresh catch would never make it to the freezer. His family loved it when he came home and put the fillets straight into the deep fryer. However, in this case the feast would have to wait. With the fillets nicely wrapped and tucked away in the freezer, Charlie picked up the bag of fish remnants from the kitchen sink and turned to walk out the back door to the garbage can to dispose of the remains. He forgot the cooler was still sitting on the floor next to him. He tripped over it, and the bag of fish skeletons, severed heads, and entrails hit the floor and burst open. The contents slid across the kitchen floor in a bloody mess.

Charlie was horrified when he stood up and ssw the scattered slimy mess. He quickly gathered it up before anyone else could see it.

Confident that he had everything bagged up again, he took it outside to the trash can. He returned to the kitchen and thoroughly cleaned and mopped the floor.

That afternoon when he drove away with his family, he was relaxed and looking forward to a wonderful vacation. He wouldn't know until five days later that something under the corner cabinet in the kitchen had been overlooked.

When the family walked into the house after the long drive back, they all immediately threw their hands over their noses and ran back outside. The house reeked of the foulest, most putrid odor they could imagine. The search for the source of the disgusting scent wasn't too hard to track down. Under the corner cabinet in the kitchen, Charlie had missed a piece of offal. As he pulled the remains of a very rotten fish head from under the cabinet, he had no choice but to admit responsibility for the stench that hung in the air like a nasty fog.

Charlie's failure to find every remnant of the dismembered fish was, of course, unintentional. Still, it resulted in a house that wasn't pleasant to come back to. Can you relate to Charlie's blunder?

Thinking of Charlie and has family entering their stinky house reminds me of a time when the Israelites failed to "clean house" thoroughly. Their error left the entire nation vulnerable to their enemies.

God was leading His people to the land He'd promised them. He was going before them and delivering their enemies into their hands. After conquering the enemies, God told the Israelites to utterly destroy anything related to the worship of pagan gods. God's people were to "tear down [the enemy's] altars, and smash their sacred pillars, and hew down their Asherim, and burn their graven images with fire" (Deuteronomy 7:5). Unfortunately, the Israelites didn't obey, which resulted in a stink, so to speak, in God's nostrils. Judges 2:1-3 records His reaction:

> The angel of the LORD came up from Gilgal to Bochim. And he said, "I brought you up out of Egypt and led you into the land which I have sworn to your fathers; and I said, 'I will never break My covenant with you, and as for you, you shall make no covenant with the inhabitants of

this land; you shall tear down their altars.' But you have not obeyed Me; what is this you have done? Therefore I also said, 'I will not drive them out before you; but they will become as thorns in your sides and their gods will be a snare to you'" (Judges 2:1-3).

What question does this passage raise in the hearts of those of us who follow Christ? Is there a leftover longing for an immoral pleasure, a drug or drink, or some other type of harmful habit that has not yet been utterly destroyed in our lives and has, therefore, become a snare to us? If so, it's time to do some housecleaning! Let's get rid of any remnants that create the terrible, rotten odor of sinfulness. The best way to start the clean-up process is through prayer!

Dear God, thank You for loving me enough to let me be totally honest with You. I admit that I've hung on to some remnants of sin I participated in or enjoyed before giving my life to You. I'm asking for Your help. Cleanse my heart of any sinfulness or action that could lead to sinfulness. I want to obey Your commands given through James, including: "Cleanse your hands, you sinners; and purify your hearts." Thank You, God, for Your mercy and grace. In the name of Your holy Son Jesus I pray, amen.

10

The Fish Gate

*Let us rise and rebuild...The Fish Gate was
rebuilt by the sons of Hassenaah.*

NEHEMIAH 2:18; 3:3

Whenever the word *fish* appears in the Scriptures, I perk up. I'm always interested to see why it is there. Today's reading mentions fish, and in this case it refers to a gate in the wall surrounding Jerusalem. I couldn't help but wonder what was important about a wall and the gates when I first read chapters 2 and 3 in Nehemiah. I discovered there are insights within this passage that are challenging and life changing.

Nehemiah was grieved when he heard that the walls of Jerusalem had not been rebuilt after King Nebuchadnezzar's attack, the deportation of the Jews to Babylon, and the subsequent return of a Jewish remnant to Jerusalem. Nehemiah knew the security, strength, and reputation of the Israelites had been jeopardized and wouldn't be restored until Jerusalem's walls were rebuilt. With permission from King Artaxerxes, whom he served as cupbearer, Nehemiah headed to Jerusalem to correct the problem. Using his well-honed skills in organization and leadership, he got the wall rebuilt in an amazing 52 days.

The account of the rebuilding of the walls in the book of Nehemiah includes the names of the gates in the wall that also needed repairs. Down through the centuries Bible teachers and scholars have compared the various gates to areas of people's lives as followers of Christ and how they need to be restored if weakened or destroyed.

The gates mentioned in the book of Nehemiah, along with symbolisms drawn from them, are what I've found helpful as I seek to stay strong in the Lord.

- *The Sheep Gate* (Nehemiah 3:1). The Sheep Gate was where the sheep were brought into the city to be sacrificed at the altar. This gate can symbolize the "Lamb of God" (Jesus) whose blood was shed on the cross for the sins of all mankind. The cross of Christ, where redemption was bought for all of us, is where we go for personal and spiritual strength—especially strength needed for rebuilding any other gate or wall in our lives that may have fallen down.

- *The Fish Gate* (verse 3). Jesus said, "Follow Me, and I will make you become fishers of men" (Mark 1:17). The Fish Gate can be a picture of where we bring people so they can be "caught" by God's grace. If this gate is broken down, it definitely needs to be rebuilt so we can continue to work with God to bring more souls into the kingdom of God.

- *The Old Gate* (verse 6). This gate can represent biblical truth. If this gate has been damaged and broken down in a person's heart, there is a danger of lies creeping in. The unshakable and everlasting truths of God must be confirmed, taught, and believed because they are the foundation for all that matters in life.

- *The Valley Gate* (verse 13). The Valley Gate can be a picture of humility of heart. When humility breaks down, pride enters in. God "opposes the proud but gives grace to the humble" (James 4:6 NIV). Developing a humble opinion of ourselves and a high opinion of God is the first step in restoring the effectiveness of this Valley Gate.

- *The Refuse Gate* (verse 14; "Dung Gate" in NIV). This gate was probably so named because outside it was where refuse from Jerusalem was dumped. This gate faced south (maybe because the wind was generally out of the north so noxious odors would blow away from Jerusalem). The Refuse Gate can represent the importance of ridding our lives of any thoughts, beliefs, and actions that aren't pleasing to God. Harmful habits and life-staining sins need to go.

- *The Fountain Gate* (verse 15). This can represent Jesus, the source of living water. Jesus said, "He who believes in Me, as the Scripture said, 'From his innermost being will flow rivers of living water'" (John 7:38). When Jesus spoke to the woman at the well, He said, "Whoever drinks of the water that I will give him shall never thirst; but the water that I will give him will become in him a well of water springing up to eternal life" (John 4:14). If the Fountain Gate has been weakened, it needs to be rebuilt so the "river of life"—Jesus Christ—can freely flow through our hearts.

- *The Water Gate* (verse 26). There is no mention in the book of Nehemiah of needed repairs to the Water Gate. We can look at the Water Gate as a symbol of the infallible Word of God. What a great picture of the fact that God's Word never breaks down and is always dependable and trustworthy. We need to always be in the Word, filling our hearts and minds with God's wisdom.

- *The Horse Gate* (verse 28). In Scripture the horse is generally associated with warfare. It is undeniable that we battle evil forces. The important fact to remember is these forces are *spiritual*. "Our struggle is not against flesh and blood, but against the rulers, against the powers, against the world forces of this darkness, against the spiritual forces of wickedness in the heavenly places" (Ephesians 6:12). If ever a broken-down gate needed mending in the life of a believer, it's this one.

- *The East Gate* (verse 29). The East Gate faced the rising sun. It provides a wonderful picture of the light of Christ that rises in our lives to dispel darkness and hopelessness.

Anyone who has stumbled or fallen under the weight of despair and pessimism needs this gate to be rebuilt in their lives.

- *The Inspection Gate* (verse 31). This gate is where military inspections were carried out. The gate can stand for judgment. Applying this to our lives, we would each do well to allow God to inspect our heart to see "if there be any hurtful way in me" (Psalm 139:24). If He points out any areas, we would be wise to ask His help in removing all that is offensive to Him.

Thank You, mighty God, for the strength-building truths in Your Word. Help me examine the walls and gates of my heart and allow You to rebuild those areas that have been weakened, damaged, and even destroyed because of sin. Thank You for Your saving and restoring grace! In Christ's precious name, amen.

Joy in the Catch

*[Jesus said,] "In the same way, I tell you, there is joy in the
presence of the angels of God over one sinner who repents."*

LUKE 15:10

Jerry's five-year-old son, Sammy, squealed excitedly when he saw the round bobber disappear and felt something yank sharply on his little fishing pole. "What do I do, Daddy?" he yelled.

His dad quickly knelt beside him and reminded him how to hold the rod tightly with one hand and work the reel with the other.

It took a few seconds for the youngster to remember what his dad had showed him, but he managed to start turning the reel handle.

"You're doing great, Sammy!" Jerry coached, smiling at his little fisherman.

Suddenly they saw a flash of silver just under the surface of the water near the bank.

"He's coming in, Sammy! Keep reeling and start backing up."

Twenty seconds later a bluegill the size of a grown man's hand was flopping in the wet grass at the pond's edge. Sammy dropped his rod and reel and jumped up and down with joy. Then he grabbed the string near the fish's mouth, held it up, and said, "Look, Daddy!"

Jerry beamed with happiness at the sight. Suddenly he realized he was missing a "Kodak moment." As he quickly dug in his pocket for his small digital camera, he said, "Sammy, keep holding your fish up. I gotta get a picture of you and your very first catch."

Sammy gladly held his pose. The smile on his face was nearly as wide as the pond behind him.

Jerry's chest swelled with fatherly pride as he snapped a couple of shots. The joy was so intense that he laughed aloud as he reviewed the photos. It was a time neither of them would ever forget.

When I picture Sammy proudly holding his fish up for his dad to photograph and Jerry's delighted reaction, I can't help but wonder if it resembles a scene that takes place between the heavenly Father and His child. I'm speaking of the moment when a Christian who has gone *fishing* on Jesus' behalf gets his or her first catch for the Lord.

I recall the first time I "reeled in" a new convert for Christ by sharing about God's saving grace. I'm well aware that God draws people to Himself through the Holy Spirit, but I was happy to be His rod and reel, so to speak. The young man who responded to the good news I shared with him was so thrilled to become a Christian that he asked me to immediately take him to the river and baptize him. It was an unforgettable experience for both of us! I'm thinking that when I stood in the water next to this new Christian and looked heavenward to pray for him before I baptized him, God was smiling at the sight. I wonder if He snapped a picture of the moment sort of like Jerry did when Sammy displayed his catch.

When we're given the opportunity to share the gospel, God is blessing us. When our sharing yields visible fruit and the person accepts Jesus Christ as their Lord and Savior, we can't help but be deeply moved. Perhaps this amazing joy is connected to what Jesus said about new believers: "There will be more joy in heaven over one sinner who repents than over ninety-nine righteous persons who need no repentance" (Luke 15:7). He also said, "I tell you, there is joy in the presence of the angels of God over one sinner who repents" (verse 10).

Jesus said to Peter and his brother, Andrew, "Follow Me, and I will make you fishers of men." May our response *always* be the same as theirs! "Immediately they left their nets and followed Him" (Matthew 4:20). He will bless our efforts so that we too will know the excitement of lifting our catch up to Him and saying, "Look, Daddy!"

God, thank You for letting me be part of Your plan to share the gospel. I'm so thankful You allow me to cast the message of Your love to the lost. And when I show my catch to You, I cherish the reality that You find joy in my efforts. Even the angels in heaven rejoice knowing another person has found Your love. I love fishing with and for You. In Christ's name I pray, amen.

He made me a fisher of men
I get a nibble every now and then
And when I do I find a brother and a brand-new friend
How blessed I am to be a fisher of men

James Alley

How Big Was It?

*They came out with all their troops and a large
number of horses and chariots—a huge army, as
numerous as the sand on the seashore.*

JOSHUA 11:4 NIV

When my son and daughter were getting close to their teen years, the three of us chartered a boat and went fishing in the Gulf of Mexico. Heidi wrestled a huge cobia (lemon fish) into the boat. When I called home to give a report to Annie about the trip. I told her about Heidi's catch.

"Babe, Heidi caught a monster fish!"

Annie was quiet for a moment and then asked, "How big was it?"

"It was as long as a surfboard!"

She silently processed what she'd just heard and, knowing the approximate size of cobia, responded graciously, "Sounds like you're having a great time."

Her reply told me she understood that my description of the catch was an attempt to explain how great the *day* of fishing had been, not just the size of the catch.

We both chuckled at my excited use of hyperbole. "Exaggeration for effect" is not uncommon. In fact, it's something most of us do even when we're not talking about fish. Likely you've heard something similar to these lines and accepted the exaggeration with good humor:

- "That limo we rode in was bigger than all outdoors!"

- "The tree that fell across the road was as tall as the Empire State Building!"
- "He was as ugly as sin!"
- "I've told you 10,000 times to clean up your room!"
- "He was faster than a speeding ticket!"

Most of us willingly accommodate statements like these that add color to our communication. There are times they help us better understand the scope of a report. Such is the case with today's verse. To give you context, here is the full passage:

> Then it came about, when Jabin king of Hazor heard of it, that he sent to Jobab king of Madon and to the king of Shimron and to the king of Achshaph, and to the kings who were of the north in the hill country, and in the Arabah—south of Chinneroth and in the lowland and on the heights of Dor on the west—to the Canaanite on the east and on the west, and the Amorite and the Hittite and the Perizzite and the Jebusite in the hill country, and the Hivite at the foot of Hermon in the land of Mizpeh. They came out, they and all their armies with them, *as many people as the sand that is on the seashore,* with very many horses and chariots. So all of these kings having agreed to meet, came and encamped together at the waters of Merom, to fight against Israel.
>
> Then the LORD said to Joshua, "Do not be afraid because of them, for tomorrow at this time I will deliver all of them slain before Israel" (Joshua 11:1-6).

The italicized words show the use of hyperbole. Any of us who have ever been to a beach know well that a two-handed scoop of beach sand contains thousands of grains of sand. Saying the armies compared in number to the sand on the seashore illustrates the gravity of the situation God's people faced.

Another instance when exaggeration was used to help the listener appreciate the impact of a report is found in Deuteronomy 1:28. The Israelite spies sent to scout Canaan reported, "The cities are large and fortified to heaven." No doubt, those who heard the description were sobered by it. The result was an even greater realization that they couldn't take the land without God on their side.

Yet another appropriate use of hyperbole is David's description of Saul and Jonathan: "They were swifter than eagles, they were stronger than lions" (2 Samuel 1:23). No man is as fast as an eagle, of course. And I don't know any man who is stronger than a lion. David was using the figure of speech hyperbole to emphasize Saul and Jonathan's valor in battle.

Finally, one of my very favorite usages of hyperbole is in a verse that describes my own life. The father of the prodigal son said to his elder son, "This brother of yours was dead and is alive again" (Luke 15:32 NIV). Obviously, the father was referring to the prodigal's spiritual condition. To some, the comparison of his son's waywardness to death might sound like an exaggeration on first hearing, but having been a prodigal myself, I understand the similarity. I can testify that the comparison of a restored relationship with the heavenly Father to being resurrected from the dead is as appropriate as can be!

Father, thank You that in many instances in Your written Word the writers were permitted to help us better understand the impact of truth more fully through the use of hyperbole. I especially appreciate hearing that You "so loved the world." I recognize that it is quite a claim indeed to say You loved absolutely everyone in the entire world, but I believe it to be true! I'm most grateful to be included in all that You love. In Christ's name, amen.

13

Dashboard Lights

The Light shines in the darkness, and the
darkness did not comprehend it.

JOHN 1:5

With a little apprehension I finally asked my wife the question I'd rehearsed for several weeks. "Don't you think it's time we get a motorboat for the family?" What Annie said in response to my suggestion was unforgettable!

"Why yes, I think it's a great idea!" she replied.

While comments like "You're a mighty handsome man" or "I'm proud of you, honey," are sweet to my ears, I'll admit that her yes answer to a motorboat made me feel all tingly inside. Needless to say, I didn't waste any time. Within a month the search for the right rig was completed, and our garage was filled with a slightly used boat we purchased from a local dealer. All we had to do was wait for spring to arrive to begin enjoying it.

During the wait for warmer weather, I totally loved going to the garage and playing with our "nused" (used but new to us) boat. I liked hooking up the water hose to the gadget that allowed me to run the motor without fear of it overheating while sitting in the driveway. And I liked sitting at the boat controls rehearsing how to throttle up and down, how to trim and tilt the engine, and how to operate the live wells that would hold the fish we'd catch. I learned everything I could about our boat—but there was an interesting feature I didn't discover until we were on the water.

Finally the weather turned warm enough for our family to take our maiden voyage. We put in at a lake on a warm, midmorning in early March. We were fully loaded with enough food and fish bait to last us until nightfall. We tooled around all day on the water, and our faces hurt from smiling. When it started getting dark, I realized we'd have to motor back to the boat ramp in the dim light of dusk.

As the sun descended behind the western end of the big lake and the darkness surrounded us, I noticed that the dashboard lights were on! With each minute of growing darkness, the brightness of the dashboard glow increased. I realized the lights had been on all day, but because of the plentiful ambient light, I hadn't noticed until darkness crept in.

Being a person who is always intrigued by the way that everyday life contains illustrations of biblical truths, I'm always on the lookout for those revelations. The dashboard lights on our boat provided a very good one.

"The Light" that is Christ is always shining! People who have invited Christ to dwell in their hearts have within them the Light that is ever burning. The interesting thing is that while He indeed shines even in the daylight of better times, like the dashboard lights on our boat, He shines more noticeably in life when darkness falls (when harder times come).

The reality of this truth was clearly seen in the spring of 2010 in Nashville. The season was progressing normally, and we welcomed the gradual warming temperatures. It was, so to speak, "daylight on the lake" for us. Then one evening the black clouds rolled in. For seemingly endless hours it rained heavily on the city and surrounding area. Floodwaters rose quickly, and without much warning thousands of families were forced from their homes and some lives were lost. Dawn came to the rest of the nation the next morning, but the citizens of Davidson County were still under the dark effects of the destruction that had come.

During this bleak time, the Light grew brighter and brighter. Like an army of love on the move, folks in the city and nearby towns who weren't affected by the raging floods poured into the streets to help others not so fortunate. The volunteers who helped ranged in age from early teens to the elderly. Annie and I thought it inspiring when we looked around and saw so many people out helping the victims of the disaster.

Where did the motivation come from to assist in the recovery? We're convinced that in a huge number of helpers the Light of compassion displayed was none other than the caring Holy Spirit. He was there all along, but the flood and resulting chaos made His light seem brighter. Nothing—not even the dark waters of a devastating flood—can put out the Light of the Holy Spirit. Blessed be the Light who always shines, especially when darkness comes!

God, thank You for dwelling in my heart in the form of the Holy Spirit. I'm grateful that His light always shines in me by day and, especially, by night. Amen.

14

Sticks in the Water

*Then [Moses] cried out to the LORD, and the
LORD showed him a tree; and he threw it into
the waters, and the waters became sweet.*

EXODUS 15:25

I was fishing off the bank of a creek in our county and the action
went from wild and frenzied one moment to a chance to sit and
soak in the sun the next. During one of the lull times, I rested my
rod in the forks of a "Y" shaped stick that I'd driven into the soft dirt
at the water's edge. As I waited for another strike I saw a small, thin,
fallen limb within arm's reach and got an idea. I picked it up, broke it
into small pieces, and gently tossed them into the water. My strategy
was to create a little surface activity that might appear to be made by
insects and, hopefully, attract hungry fish to the area around my bait.
I thought my idea was rather clever. Even though I can't prove that it
was the cause, the fishing action picked up after the "sticks in the water"
tactic. It turned out to be a fun and productive day of fishing.

Not long ago while at Sunday church, the pastor delivered a message that made me think of what I'd done at the creek's edge. The passage was from the book of Exodus:

> Then Moses led Israel from the Red Sea, and they went
> out into the wilderness of Shur; and they went three days
> in the wilderness and found no water. When they came to
> Marah, they could not drink the waters of Marah, for they
> were bitter; therefore it was named Marah. So the people
> grumbled at Moses saying, "What shall we drink?" Then

he cried out to the LORD, and the LORD showed him a tree; and he threw it into the waters, and the waters became sweet (15:22-25).

The lesson the pastor drew from the reading was inspiring to say the least. He pointed out that the Israelites had already faced the challenge of having their backs against the wall…er…river…when it looked like the Egyptians had them cornered at the Red Sea—but God delivered them. Now on the other side of the Red Sea, their need for water wasn't met for three painful days. And when they finally reached water, it was bitter and undrinkable. The people grumbled, and that's when Moses cried out to God once again for His intervention. God heard him and showed him a tree. When he threw a branch into the bitter water, the liquid became sweet and consumable.

The pastor went on to say that because Christ is the central theme of the Scriptures, everything in the Bible points to Him. The Exodus passage is no exception. The tree (wood) that was thrown into the bitter waters of Marah can be viewed as representing the cross of Christ. When Jesus enters the waters of our lives that have been made bitter by sin, He redeems us and makes life sweet, nourishing, refreshing, and hopefully a blessing to others.

I doubt Moses actually knew what a powerful illustration of hope his actions would yield that day when he tossed the wood into the bitter waters. Likely, he was simply being obedient in the moment. And for sure he didn't know that thousands of years later a Tennessee fisherman would glean something from it that is so incredibly meaningful.

The next time you're fishing at the edge of a creek or pond and get the urge to toss some wood into the water, go ahead and do it—and remember Jesus and what He did for you on the cross at Calvary.

O mighty God, thank You for what Jesus accomplished on the cross on my behalf. How wonderful that when He enters the water of my life, sweetness enters with Him. Blessed be His holy name! In Jesus' beautiful name I pray, amen.

15

No Fishing

I will remember their sins no more.

HEBREWS 8:12

Kevin and Gregg were casting their spinner baits into the lake on opposite sides of the boat. As they did, they enjoyed doing something that goes very well with two old friends and fishing—talking. The conversation trail they followed went from recalling some of the friends they grew up with to reminding each other of some of the mischief they got into as youngsters. They moved on to the girls they'd dated and were glad they never married and then to some of their favorite song lyrics.

Eventually the subject of something that happened when they were both 21 came up. Kevin got quiet for a few seconds and then admitted, "I've really tried to push the wreck out of my memory, but we both know it doesn't work."

Gregg cast his line again and didn't say anything for a few minutes. He knew exactly what Kevin was referring to because he'd been there when it happened. Ten years earlier they were both under the influence of alcohol and on the road. Kevin was driving the pickup and crossed the centerline. The resulting head-on crash severely injured the young driver of the other vehicle. Though she survived, it took her months to recover. Kevin and Gregg's injuries were relatively minimal. Except for Kevin's slightly gimpy shoulder and a scar over Gregg's left eye, no one would know they'd been hurt.

It wasn't the first time the conversation between the two friends had come to a halt because of the unwelcome memory. Neither of them had dealt very well with the guilt they felt for being so reckless. However, a change had come into their lives that helped them regain a level of peace in their hearts. In their thirties, they'd become followers of Jesus Christ.

Among the sins they confessed, the regretful drunkenness that had resulted in such great harm to the young lady was highest on the list. With great contrition they prayed for forgiveness. Gregg seemed to be a little more accepting of God's total pardon, but Kevin struggled to believe he was fully forgiven. For that reason, he was quicker to bypass any conversation about the incident. But that day in the boat, Gregg had an encouraging word to offer that could help them both.

He let a few minutes pass as they continued to quietly fish. Then he said, "Kevin, I know you still hurt in your heart over what happened on the highway all those years ago. I do too. I guess it wouldn't really be right if we didn't feel so bad about it. I'm glad we went to the young woman and asked for her forgiveness. I know we're both grateful she gave it. But you've told me time and again that it's still the one thing you can't seem to feel total forgiveness for from God. I understand what you're saying, but I heard something the other day that might help."

Kevin offered a careful, "And what was that?"

Gregg reeled slowly. "My pastor was talking about God's complete forgiveness. Among the things he said was, 'Don't forget that God has cast our sins into the sea of forgetfulness, and He put up a "No Fishing" sign. God doesn't want those of us who have sins in *that* sea to go fish them out. It's done, they're gone, and that's it.'"

With a compassionate tone, Gregg added, "Buddy, I for one needed to hear what the pastor said. Truth is, we're both doing more than fishing for smallmouth bass today. Once again we've dropped our lines into the sea that God doesn't want us fishing in. Don't you think it's time to reel in our line and put the tackle away?"

A full minute passed before Kevin finally responded. "If I don't catch anything else today, that's something I will take home and chew on."

Gregg knew his friend well enough to know that he'd heard what was shared and took it to heart. He smiled and offered a little more encouragement. "Let's help each other heed the 'No Fishing' sign. We're never gonna forget what we did, but because of God's grace and forgiveness, we can remember it without the pain."

Dear God, from the depths of my heart I thank You for Your heart and wisdom shared in Psalm 103:12: "As far as the east is from the west, so far [have You] removed our transgressions from us." May You be forever praised for Your love that is so great. In Christ's name, amen.

16

The Inescapable Net

Like fish caught in a treacherous net...

ECCLESIASTES 9:12

Back in the 1960s, whenever my friend and I needed some minnows to use for bait we didn't need to spend our hard-earned nickels to buy them at the local bait shop. Instead, we grabbed our homemade seining net and headed to the creek that ran behind our neighborhood. We could catch all the little swimmers we needed!

The cold water would take our breath away as we stepped into the knee-deep stream and put the top half of the eight-foot-long, tightly webbed net under the surface. We would then push it down to the bed of the creek with the end poles. Working together to keep the net stretched as wide as possible and touching the muddy bottom, we would work our way upstream and then sweep the net to the bank so the tiny fish had nowhere to go.

As we lifted the net out of the water, we both gave satisfied grins as we looked bug-eyed at the flopping, free bait we'd trapped. After emptying our catch in our minnow bucket, we'd repeat the process at least a half dozen times. With each submerged sweep of our net, the collection of bait would grow. And so did our anticipation for catching some sizable bass with our very active, live lures.

As fun as it was to get into the creek and capture our bait, there was something about the process that generated a bit of remorse in me. I never did reveal it to my friend, but I felt a little sorry for the miniature fish we corralled. As they were suddenly scooped up out of their natural habitat and wiggled wildly in the net, I couldn't help but think what fear they must be feeling.

Of course, the regret I felt about their sad state wasn't enough to motivate me to put them back into the creek. The possibility that they would entice a weighty rod-bender to my hook when my buddy and I dropped them into the waters of the bass-filled pond where we were going to fish overrode any inclination to show them mercy. Still, I won't forget those momentary sensations of sorrow I felt on their behalf.

One day, years later, I was reading in the book of Ecclesiastes. I came across this part of a verse: "Like fish caught in a treacherous net" (9:12). When I read those words, my thoughts went back to the minnows that were trapped in our homemade seine. What bewilderment they must have felt when they were swimming along, feeling safe in the creek, when suddenly they noticed a dreadful wall. And when the net touched them and pushed them into an inescapable corner, they must have been terrified.

They weren't aware that their fate included being manhandled by two young boys, being impaled in their midsections by sharp hooks, and likely being swallowed by a bigger fish. All they knew when they were flopping in the net was that one moment all was well and in the next their world had fallen apart.

The sudden terror that came upon the minnows is what Ecclesiastes 9:12 is referring to. After the minnows, the same verse mentions "birds trapped in a snare." Unfortunately, this verse isn't just about fish and birds. Ultimately, it refers to you and me. The full verse reads:

> Moreover, man does not know his time: like fish caught in
> a treacherous net and birds trapped in a snare, so the sons
> of men are ensnared at an evil time when it suddenly falls
> on them.

Many of us have lived long enough to know how true this verse is. From a tornado that unexpectedly tears through a town in the middle of the night to a derailed train that wreaks havoc on a subdivision, from the horror of seeing a semi careening across the median toward another car to being robbed at gunpoint, the examples of the sudden terror we face are plenty. Untold numbers of us have found ourselves unable to escape as we're instantly pushed through the waters of life by the tight net of tragedy. It's a reality we'd rather not think about, yet it happens.

The question this unavoidable truth brings to mind is, "What are we to do with the fact that the net of calamity can appear anytime?" The answer is found two verses earlier, in Ecclesiastes 9:10: "Whatever your hand finds to do, do it with all your might; for there is no activity or planning or knowledge or wisdom in Sheol [the grave] where you are going."

The writer of Ecclesiastes recognizes that we're all headed to the minnow bucket, so to speak. Because this is true, it would be wise for us to redeem the time by going for broke when it comes to doing whatever we're doing with our lives. Whether we're husbands, wives, parents, doctors, preachers, salespeople, musicians, teachers, editors, soldiers, or any other role life has to offer, we need to fulfill it to the best of our ability. We need to do the thing we know how to do—and do it full bore—until the moment the net pulls us out of the waters of life. This includes being fishermen!

God, thank You for giving me time on this earth to enjoy life. I'm very aware that it can abruptly end, so I'm asking You to help me redeem my days by showing me how to be the best at whatever You want my hands to do. In Christ's name, amen.

17

The Working Worm

Be of sober spirit, be on the alert. Your adversary,
the devil, prowls around like a roaring lion,
seeking someone to devour.

1 PETER 5:8

One of the best sources for good fish bait is right behind my house. Especially in the wet spring seasons, the backyard teems with several species of worms. From red wigglers to nightcrawlers, the opportunity to quickly and easily fill up a container with a half-day's worth of fish food makes going out even more enjoyable.

I won't forget the morning I encountered a moment of compassion for one of the worms. As I sat on my patio overlooking our freshly mowed lawn, something caught my eye about 15 yards away. A robin landed in the dew-covered short grass and scoured the ground for its breakfast. Suddenly, the bird stopped, buried its beak into the grass, and pulled its head sharply backward. In its jaws I could see a worm stretched tight. With a few quick bobs of its head, the skillful robin managed to capture a mouthful of juicy invertebrate.

As it flew away with the two-and-a-half-inch victim dangling from its mouth, I couldn't help but think of a well-known proverb: "The early bird gets the worm." I pondered the sight and, for a fleeting minute or two, was inspired to examine my own level of industriousness. After all, that's the effect the old bit of wisdom is supposed to have. However, I saw another way to look at the picture.

What about the poor worm? It was minding its own business, out doing its job of aerating the ground, when suddenly it was under attack, pinched in the powerful grip of the bird's beak. It must have constricted fiercely in an attempt to hold on to the turf. Overcome by a creature of greater strength, the worm let go and met its demise. *How sad,* I thought.

Sympathy gave birth to a new proverb that day. It asks, "If the early bird gets the worm, wouldn't it pay the worm to sleep in?" Had it slumbered just a little longer, its life would have been spared (and my lawn would not have lost another caretaker). However, the little guy, like most of us, had to yield to the need for making a living by getting up and going to work. There's hardly any way to avoid it. That being true, the only possible solution for vulnerable creatures like worms would be to go forth with an attitude of alertness. It should be listening for the rustle of feet in the grass. It must keep an eye out for a shadow that warns it of the peril that looms above. Not only are there feathered monsters who would eat it, there are also hook-happy humans who go stalking for fish fodder.

Wouldn't we all do well to enter our places of business with a watchful attitude? As we venture into the "daily grind," we should be on guard against dangers—especially those that would harm the heart. If we fail to do so we might end up becoming a meal! Deception, theft, laziness, and gossip may be invading the very place where we labor, attempting to consume us.

Consider the strong words of caution found in today's verse. Since most of us can't hide ourselves away in our dwellings and avoid contact with a sometimes cruel world, may we leave the safety of our homes with an ear to the ground and an eye to the sky. In Psalm 56:6, David said of the enemy that pursued him, "They attack, they lurk, they watch my steps, as they have waited to take my life." The same could be said of how the devil seeks his victims. He lays in wait for you and me.

Being alert is an important part of defense. Like the worm, we might not be able to sleep in, but we should certainly watch out!

Blessed Father in heaven, keeper of my soul, sustain me today with a sober spirit. Help me be on guard against the evil one who would consume me. Help me see the subtle warnings of danger when the devil comes near. I know I must run to You when it happens, so Lord, help me stay close to You today. In Jesus' name I pray, amen.

18

Remember the Sabbath

*Let us consider how to stimulate one another to love and
good deeds, not forsaking our own assembling together,
as is the habit of some, but encouraging one another;
and all the more as you see the day drawing near.*

HEBREWS 10:24-25

Remember the Sabbath day to keep it holy.

EXODUS 20:8

I am a man who passionately loves the outdoors. If I had a choice
between eating a scrumptious, expensive meal inside a big city restaurant or sitting on a creek bank with half a peanut butter sandwich, I
would opt for a little bite of food and a big piece of the sky. While my
admitted obsession with being "out there" might be better than other
vices, an unbridled affection for enjoying nature has its drawbacks.
One particularly negative side effect is often revealed in my heart when
a springtime Sunday morning rolls around.

Here in our neck of the planet, crappie fishing season gets underway when the air starts to warm—sometime in April or May. Making
an early-morning stop at the local bait shop to buy two- or three-dozen
minnows, a few fresh, colorful jigs, and filling the Thermos with some
hot coffee to wash down the donuts is a pleasure beyond description.
Mornings like that are one of the main ingredients God uses to draw
us closer to Him and His creation.

While it is difficult on any day of the week to wake up and not head
to the lake, it is especially hard on Sunday mornings. Being one who

believes firmly it is God who created the outdoors that we enjoy, I am also convinced that He designated a day when His followers should gather and corporately worship Him. As I leave my driveway and turn toward the church instead of the lake, the battle in my heart begins.

As I head down the highway, I pass pickups pulling trailers loaded with boats. Sticking up just above the railing of those fiberglass and aluminum shrines I see the bouncing tips of rods ready for reeling. I can't see them, but I know on the floors of those vessels there are coolers filled with canned drinks and snacks waiting to be consumed with a smile. The thought of it hurts. I'm almost offended that the owners of the boats take a route that taunts me with the temptation to turn around and follow them. How rude!

As the anglers go by, I look into their faces. Don't they know their smiles disturb my piety? Can't they see how anxious I am at the thought that they will be catching fish that won't be there for me to hook on Monday morning? What's wrong with these people? But as I drive ahead and silently rant and rave, it usually doesn't take long before Someone speaks words to my heart that sting the flesh: "You shall have no other gods before Me" (Exodus 20:3). And then I argue (as if I could win), "Respectfully, I submit that it was You who made me a man who hears the call of the wild. I am only responding to my nature."

Whenever I present my puny ideas, God's silence says much more than I want to hear. All He has to do is wait for me to feel sufficiently guilty for my lame excuse for my obsession with the outdoors. My idols are real. And they offend God when Sabbath days come around and I want to do anything but gather with other believers to recognize and honor Him. If I care for my relationship with Him more than anything else in this world, I know I must work on curbing my will, bringing it under God's control.

There are some who rarely, if ever, choose the pew over perching on the bow of their boats on Sunday mornings. Their argument is often, "Worshiping God is best done out in His creation!" If that assertion is consistently used as their excuse to avoid church, they should understand that it's a claim that holds water about as well as a boat that's lost its drain plug.

Even as I struggle emotionally when watching others make their way merrily to the lake, I know that ahead of me, inside the sanctuary, is the joy of obedience. And that, my friend, is a good catch!

Thank You, Father, for making the Sabbath. It is the governor of passions for people like me who love to be outside. I pray for the courage to always choose to be with my fellow believers as often as possible. You are worthy to be praised—far more than what You made. In Jesus' name, amen.

19

Catch and Release

While I was with them,
I was keeping them in Your name.

John 17:12

I had lived a long time when I first heard about a method of fishing called "catch and release." The idea had been around a while, I'm sure, but somehow it had gotten by me.

My introduction to this tactic took place in Colorado in 1987. I was invited to attend a board meeting and men's retreat for a large ministry and provide the music. Included in the fun activities for the attendees was the opportunity to fly-fish for trout in a nearby stream. Having had limited experience with gently laying a fly on the water, I was anxious to try my hand at it. *And* I could almost taste the fried version of the catch I hoped to take home.

When I went to the tackle office to get my rod and reel and selection of tied flies I was met with a surprise. The first fly I picked from the fancy case was beautifully tied. As I examined it I noticed a flaw.

"Excuse me," I said to the man behind the half-door counter, "I believe there's something wrong with this fly. It seems to be missing the barb."

The fellow was kind as he smiled slightly and announced, "Oh! Perhaps you were not aware, but we have a catch-and-release policy here at the lodge."

I know the expression on my face did not hide my bewilderment.

"What's the point in that?" I asked softly in order to not reveal my ignorance to the other folks in the lobby area.

"Well," the man said in too loud a voice, "we want to protect the trout population and preserve them for future guests."

I was dumbfounded and he knew it. With a puzzled look stuck on my face, I pinned a few of the faulty flies on my vest and went through with the trip to the river. I managed to land a couple of nice fish and, with some reluctance, let them go back to their pools with slightly disfigured lips.

Where I was raised in West Virginia, the idea of hooking a big bass or catfish, cranking it to the bank, admiring it, then letting it go was not part of our lifestyle. Most of us had a different idea: catch it, dress it, bless it, and consume it. And between the dressing and the blessing was an enjoyable event we called a fish fry. The fellowship that went along with the aroma of boiling peanut oil with battered fish nuggets dancing on top would make any angler scoff at the catch-and-release concept.

I have come to accept the fact that there are good reasons for catching fish and then releasing them. Letting healthy fish live and multiply and supporting endangered species are two good goals. The downside, however, is that it puts the emphasis on the fun, not the food. To focus on the enjoyable challenge of the catch while avoiding the seriousness of taking a life could promote a disregard for causing suffering.

Whether you agree or not, let me take a leaping liberty with the catch-and-release idea. In it is a picture of something that should never happen for those of us who embrace the Great Commission of soul fishing. To net them, admire them, then let them swim back into the waters of the world would not be a good thing. The work that follows the catch is very much part of the deal. In Matthew 28 take careful note that verse 20, which says, "Teaching them to observe all that I commanded you," follows right after the charge in verse 19 to "go therefore and make disciples." Seeing that hooking them then overlooking them is not the way of the Word, it would be safe to assume that when it comes to fishing for people, God promotes "catch and keep"!

Lord, thank You that I was caught and am being kept by Your Holy Spirit. And thank You for those who have been faithful to attend to me after I was landed in the net of Your grace. In Jesus' name, amen.

20

"OK, Step One!"

You have need again for someone to teach you.

HEBREWS 5:12

U ntil I moved to Tennessee in 1974, my fishing had been limited to throwing a line from the banks of farm ponds and the shores of the Ohio River. I also had some brief experiences with standing in a trout stream and tying myself into knots. Never had I ventured onto the waters in a boat.

In the Nashville area there are two nice lakes. Old Hickory and Percy Priest are a wonderful pair of opportunities for those who enjoy big lake fishing. When I was told that the coves where an angler could find solitude and success were nearly innumerable, I longed to drop a line into them. However, to get to them you had to have a boat—unless you didn't mind some long, long walks. Because I didn't own a vessel or know anyone who did, I could only dream about getting out there…until I heard about the rentals at Elm Hill Marina.

It was said that the office at Elm Hill would make available a 14-foot aluminum rig to anyone willing to fork out their hard-earned bucks. The idea rolled around in my head for weeks. The one thing that kept me from going straightaway to the marina was not the money. It was the fact that I didn't have the first clue on how to operate a motorized boat.

It must have been the extra strong coffee that day, but one morning I decided to drive out to Percy Priest and make my dreams come true. I walked into the little office, plopped down my money, and signed the papers. Within minutes I was walking down the dock behind the rental agent. The next thing I knew the motor was puttering in neutral. (Fortunately, the agent had to start the engine to make sure it was operating well enough for a day's workout. I didn't have a clue for firing it up.)

Satisfied the motor would be fine, the fellow stepped out of the boat and said, "Turn the handle counterclockwise to go forward and clockwise to reverse. Have a nice day. See you at four this afternoon." With that far-too-brief lesson, I climbed in and sat down in front of the engine. I had at least seen enough pictures to know where I was supposed to sit. Other than that, I was at a loss.

My hands shook as I rolled the throttle into reverse. Well...I thought I was putting it into reverse. I had overlooked the fact that when facing forward, one has to think backward to work their hands behind them. *"Bang!"* Up against the dock I plowed. Quickly I rolled the handle the other way, and I shot across the water like a surface torpedo. I was heading straight for a huge, beautiful sailboat. I jerked the handle sideways and barely missed the hull of the tall boat. Then I heard a scream.

I'm not sure how it happened, but I was going almost at full throttle in reverse right at a brand-new ski boat. The lady aboard was frantic and her voice screeched as she yelled, *"No! Get away!"* At that I reversed the roll of the throttle, and by the grace of heaven I just missed a lawsuit. One more coat of wax on their boat and I would have been financially sunk right there.

The agent must have heard the commotion above the country music blaring on his radio because he appeared in a flash. As he approached the dock nearest to me, he was immediately aware that he had rented his boat to a complete novice (a nice way of saying "idiot"). I'll never forget how exasperated he sounded when he threw his cigarette into the water and said, "OK, step one!" With the skill of a seasoned mariner, in just a few brief moments of instructions on the basics, he had me on my way to the coves I had dreamed about. Though it started with the ingredients for a nightmare, the day turned out quite nice.

I admit it was not smart to board that boat with no training whatsoever. To expect to go from an unenlisted sailor straight to the captain's chair is a stunt no swabbie would ever try. How grateful I was for the rental agent's willingness to teach me the basics.

In our walk with Christ, it is important to understand that there are also foundational steps to following Him. Hebrews 5:12 refers to them as "the elementary principles of the oracles of God." While the first verse of the next chapter informs us that pressing on to maturity should be our goal, we must remember that there are basics to be grasped. A willingness to learn them is paramount to being an effective worker for the Lord. Learning the basics is the key to avoiding the damage to the "hull of other hearts" as well as our own.

Lord, thank You for Your divine patience in teaching me the basics. Help me embrace them and move on to deeper waters. In Jesus' name, amen.

21

The Rudder

From the same mouth come both blessing and cursing.

JAMES 3:10

Without a doubt, the largest boat from which I ever fished was the aircraft carrier *USS Forrestal/CVA-59*. While many considered it a vessel of defense and a floating airport that housed upwards of 5000 men and an unbelievable inventory of planes and support equipment, I saw it as my personal deep-sea fishing rig. I simply let a lot of people use it for things like launching F-4 Phantom fighter jets and such.

Seriously, when I wasn't dropping a line off the side in various harbors where we docked, I was admiring the incredible mass of metal. Though now decommissioned, it once sailed proudly displacing approximately 80,000 tons! Its size was absolutely staggering. The flight and hangar decks alone covered 325,000 square feet! I couldn't help but marvel that something so huge and heavy could be buoyant. Yet it was, and its designers and crew had my utmost respect.

I'll never forget the day I was permitted to descend into the canyon of the dry dock where the *Forrestal* was sitting. A six-month refurbishing was underway in Portsmouth, Virginia, and my curiosity to see the underside of the great ship drove me to request a walk below its hull. I'll be forever grateful that I was allowed to do so.

I didn't realize so much of the ship was designed to be underwater, unseen by onlookers who viewed only its stately silhouette against the horizon. The height from keel to mast was 25 stories. Its length, approximately 1039 feet, was so extensive that I could not see the stern while standing beneath the bow. Its massive weight sat solidly on the huge supports that hugged its hull.

With hard hat strapped securely on my head so it wouldn't fall off while I gazed upward, I slowly walked the distance of the open pit. The ship was breathtaking to behold. My admiration for its existence and the people who built it escalated with every step. I finally reached the aft section and the sight of the four 5-blade screws (propellers) that pushed the gray monster was mind-boggling. I stood motionless, stunned at the sight.

What I saw next was perhaps the most astonishing part of the tour. Hanging down from the hull, each about the size of a pair of jumbo American flags that are flown at Tennessee's state capitol building, were the ship's three rudders. What amazed me was the fact that such a gargantuan vessel could be directed by relatively small devices. When compared to the overall size of the ship, it didn't seem possible. Yet, when turned by the captain's wheel, they could dictate the direction of the "city at sea."

With so much influence by so little mass, it is no wonder that rudders get the honor of being mentioned in the Scriptures. The maritime irony they represent is used as a picture of the effect of the human tongue in the third chapter of the book of James: "Look at the ships also, though they are so great and are driven by strong winds, are still directed by a very small rudder wherever the inclination of the pilot desires. So also the tongue is a small part of the body, and yet it boasts of great things" (verses 4-5).

Humans are not unlike the great seagoing vessels. As our "ships" sail the waters of relationships, storms will sometimes arise and we must carefully navigate our way. During those times especially, we will be far better off if we give rudder control to our worthy Captain. Letting Christ steer our conversations will ensure our safe and successful passage through troubled waters.

Father, I am grateful You have given me the ability to communicate. Help me exercise control of it so that the destination to which I sail will be a peaceful harbor. Forgive me for those times I allowed the strong winds of adversity to rip the helm from my hands. I lean on You for the strength and wisdom to guide this vessel. In Jesus' holy name, amen.

22

First Fish

Take the first fish that comes up.

MATTHEW 17:27

One of my most valued possessions is a black-and-white photo taken in 1956. It's one of those things I hope I have time to grab if I were suddenly forced to escape a house fire. It speaks of a day I will forever cherish, and to lose the picture would be a personal tragedy.

What's in the snapshot? It's me as a little boy standing on the muddy bank of a small farm pond in West Virginia behind the country home of Robert and Rose Duty. In one hand is a cane fishing pole and in the other is the thin line. Hanging on the hook is my very first fish, a tiny bluegill! My smile of excitement is obvious but not huge. I seem happy about catching something but scared of what I held hostage. It appears as though I were wondering, "This is really neat, but what do I do now?" Like a bookmark in the pages of my past, this black-and-white treasure is a testimony of my introduction to the world of angling.

Whenever I reflect on that important day in my life, I often recall the mention of another "first fish" in the writings of the New Testament. It is found in the book of Matthew: "However, so that we do not offend them, go to the sea and throw in a hook, and take the first fish that comes up; and when you open its mouth, you will find a shekel. Take that and give it to them for you and Me" (Matthew 17:27).

Inside that well-known fish was something of great value to both Jesus and Peter. It was a coin sufficient to meet their need for the taxes they would voluntarily pay in order to placate the collectors. How the coin got there is anybody's guess. Perhaps the fish picked it up during feeding. The point is, it was not the fish the two men needed—it was what was *inside* it.

There's a picture of life in that miraculous catch that would be good for parents of very young children to observe. A first fish, like the one I caught, is more than a floppy, slimy, smelly slab of scales and fins. Inside that fish, so to speak, is something that can meet a need far more important than paying a tax. The time spent together in the wonders of the great outdoors is a priceless treasure children can hold on to. As a result of the excitement of feeling the tug and pull of landing that initial fish, children can get hooked on an activity that can eventually encourage them to discover similar opportunities for spending time with their own kids!

It only took a couple of trips to the water with my little kids and fishing gear for me to realize, "If you want to be with your kids, take them fishing…but, if you want to go fishing, don't take the kids." The sacrifice of much-needed solitude (and safety as well, since those wildly flying hooks on a child's line can hurt a fellow) was worth the return I experienced. As a result of catching their first fish with dad standing by, I have two grown children who are my friends as much as they are my offspring. Our closeness has value beyond measure because it meets an incredibly important need—time spent together in love!

Thank You, Father, for creating a world full of wonder. In it You have supplied every need, including ponds and streams filled with fish so parents and children can make unforgettable memories. Blessed be Your name, amen.

23

The Battle Cry

Who will stand up for me against evildoers?
Who will take his stand for me against those who do
wickedness? If the LORD had not been my help, my
soul would soon have dwelt in the abode of silence.

PSALM 94:16-17

The marina was well-equipped with a wide boat ramp and fueling station. As my brother-in-law, Bill, and I prepared the 17-foot fish/ski combo for launching, another boat slowly approached the area. It was a sleek ski boat that featured a center deck engine cover.

Annie and her sister, Gail, stood on shore and monitored the kids as they played in knee-deep water. Bill and I were nearly ready to back the trailer down the ramp. About 75 feet away, where the other boat had moored to the dock, there suddenly appeared on the engine cover the nearly naked body of a woman.

Apparently she intended to get a tan on parts of her derriere, so she perched herself on all fours with her backside facing the sky. The "thong" style bikini didn't cover quite enough to qualify for decency. Bill and I encouraged one another to keep our attention focused on our jobs.

We were not the only ones who were aware of the scene, however. Our wives, two sisters known for not withholding their thoughts about social ills, also saw the skin show. Annie stood completely silent and puzzled at the thought that anyone would ever wear such an uncomfortable item.

Gail, on the other hand, was not quiet that day. When she saw the "shiny hiney" on that engine cover and realized her son and husband (and brother-in-law) might stumble at the scene, without hesitation she yelled her feelings across the water. And the quiet cove carried her voice like a rock-and-roll band's sound system. Her statement left us all shocked: *"Excuse me! Your butt's in the air!"*

As the announcement of the obvious echoed loudly across the cove, the embarrassed sunbather slid off the engine cover and onto the floor of the boat. Annie started laughing uncontrollably and struggled to say, "Dear sister, I can't believe you said that!"

Without batting a conservative eye, Gail responded, "If she has the nerve to show it, I have the nerve to tell her I see it!"

While many in the area may not have classified the showing of one's exposed rear as a terribly immoral act, Gail viewed it differently. Indecency was not to be tolerated. As wild and unexpected as it was, her bold assessment of the situation literally changed all of our lives. As a result of her brave words, Annie and I find ourselves more ready and willing to stand up for righteousness. Several times since, we have looked at one another when we're appalled at some social corruption taking place in our presence and uttered the battle cry, "Excuse me, your butt's in the air!" With that as our emotional catapult, we then challenge what's wrong.

Today's verse speaks to this issue and is as much a warning to us as it is a confession. Oh! How I don't want to live in a weak, cowardly abode of silence. Instead, I long to be a man who can raise my voice when needed to remind a fallen world that a stand is taken against unrighteousness. I want to be brave enough to say, "If they have the nerve to show it, I have the nerve to tell them I see it!" How about you?

God, how thankful I am that You have ordained righteousness.
Help me to not only pursue it but also to fight for it. I pray for
the courage to speak up when it is time to do so and not be found
hiding in the shadows of silence. In Jesus, Your brave Son's name,
I pray, amen.

24

Old Fishing Boats

God makes a home for the lonely.

PSALM 68:6

Sadness washed over me when I saw it sitting in our neighbor's backyard. The old fishing boat had been there when we first moved in the summer of 1988, and it was still in the same spot when we moved away in 1996. I'm not sure how long it sat in the yard before we arrived, but the sight of it tore at me each time I took it in.

The craft was an olive-green aluminum boat. As a result of its long stay in the shadows of the trees, it was covered with sap and mildew. The many Spring seasons had brought new crops of leaves and many Autumns dumped them into the unused boat. The flat tires of the trailer were buried in the dirt, and grass had overtaken the axles. What a pitiful scene it was.

We were unable to get to know the owners of the boat. We knew their names and a few other items about them, but that was about it. As far as their relationship with their lonely boat was concerned, I assumed it was a "toy" the family had enjoyed for a while. I couldn't be sure. But one thing was for certain, there was a day when they brought it home from the marine dealer and proudly parked it in their yard. They probably even peeked through the window blinds that evening and dreamed of the fun it represented.

I also suspect there was good care given at first to the old boat. A cleaning cloth probably slid faithfully across its hull after it was retrailered and brought back home from the lake. The carpet was likely vacuumed. The drain plug was pulled so it would empty of residual water. The required maintenance was done to keep the small outboard motor in good running order. The prized possession was likely treated as one of the family until one day something began to change. Perhaps the kids grew up and their interest in going fishing waned. As a result, the boat sat longer and longer between trips to the water. Maybe the dad got too busy maintaining a living. At some unknown point in time there was a lifelessness about the boat out back that became unnoticed.

Admitting there is still enough "little kid" left in me to humanize inanimate things, I imagined the old fishing boat might have had something to say about its sad state. Feeling quite lonely, it may have wakened and spoke each time it heard our neighbor's lawn mower start up. "Aha! They're mowing the yard today. Maybe they'll see me and pull me out of this mud hole to take me to the lake. There I'll see friends I haven't seen for so long. And, oh, how I long to feel the water flowing across my belly again. Perhaps today!" But it wasn't to be. Day after day, summer after summer, year after year the time passed until the old boat was completely forgotten. Ignored by its family, it lowered its bow one evening and died.

When I came along, what I saw was not just an old, dilapidated aluminum boat. It was a haunting reminder of some folks I've seen in my day. At one time they were valued and felt a usefulness that kept them energized and shipshape. Then somewhere along the path of time, they were forgotten. Others around them got distracted by life. Eventually, they were left only with hope that people would come along, find them worthy of their attention, and give them a home where they would be loved and appreciated.

Most of us do not have to look very far to find an "old vessel" whose spirit is barely alive. They are around us, some right in our own homes. Perhaps it's time to go to them and see if they can be encouraged.

Father, I'm glad You have ways of reminding me to reach out to those people who need a friend. Help me to see the old boats around me, especially those in my neighborhood. Show me how to encourage and restore their joy. In Jesus' name, amen.

25

Born for Adversity

A friend loves at all times,
and a brother is born for adversity.

PROVERBS 17:17

My friend Jon has a part-time job as a scuba diver for the emergency rescue and recovery team in his county. He had finished his regular day's work with the state game commission and was on his way home for the evening when the radio in his truck broke the silence.

"Jon, we need you to bring your gear and join us for a drowning search."

He quickly responded and asked for directions and information about the victim.

The voice on the other end of the radio replied, "Jon, there are two of them, a set of twins."

Saddened by the thought of the accident and the parents' grief, Jon turned his pickup around and headed to the location of the tragedy. About ten minutes before reaching the scene the radio sounded again.

"Jon, the victims have been found. You can head home if you like."

He acknowledged the call and turned his vehicle homeward. When he arrived at work the next morning, he called the emergency unit's office to check on the incident. He asked a fellow diver, "How about the parents of the little boys? I assume they are really torn up about this."

The answer to his question left Jon completely stunned. "Little boys? Jon, these twins were 84 years old! They were fishing together and somehow their boat capsized."

As Jon hung up the phone his heart filled with a mixture of feelings. He was deeply sorrowed by the thought of the two elderly gentlemen struggling in the water to survive. Only God knows the level of terror they must have experienced. Jon also thought of those who knew and loved the men. What incredibly bitter tears they must be shedding because of the loss. Among the emotions that gripped his heart, admiration was especially strong. Jon thought about the fact that two brothers, who had traveled side by side for so many miles down the road of life, were still friends enough to want to go fishing together. Something about their relationship caused them to maintain a unity that spanned two generations of time. What a testimony to the power of brotherhood!

Today's verse accurately describes the elderly twins who had lived and died together. How sweet it is to be able to count on the help and support of a brother or sister when life deals a painful blow. How sad it is for those who cannot turn to someone during hard times.

I am a brother to one sister. Sometimes I resent what time and distance have done to our ability to connect. Living several hundred miles apart for so long has reduced our fellowship to an occasional holiday visit or a brief phone call. Yet I love my sister deeply, and I'm willing to go to her side if serious trouble invades her life.

Several years ago, our son, Nathan, wrote the following lyric for his sister, Heidi. He couldn't afford a birthday gift so, as an alternative, he wrote the following words. They are priceless:

> Here's to my sister
> Remember every day
> No matter what I've said
> Here's what I'd like to say
> I will always love you
> Be with you to the end
> When no one else is around
> I will be your friend
> I love my sister
> And I always will
> I'm proud to be your brother
> That's how I feel

And someday when you're far away
And the miles keep us apart
I'm gonna whisper
"I love my sister"
And you'll know it in your heart.

Today would be a good day to reach out and touch the heart of a sibling you have not spoken to in a while. Why wait for adversity to motivate you to tell someone you love them? Call now!

God, You are good to give us siblings. Thank You for the encouragement we can be to one another. Help me be a comfort in times of adversity. In Jesus' name, amen.

26

We Remember the Fish

We remember the fish which we used to eat free in Egypt.

NUMBERS 11:5

If you were to ask my daughter, Heidi, about the fish we have caught and consumed, I think I know which two she might say were the best. It would be a tie between the halibut in Canada and the king mackerel landed off the coast of Florida. When fresh fish tastes as good as it did on the evenings after we caught and grilled them, there is no way we could ever forget. Even now our taste buds stand at attention at the memory.

The incredible edible experiences like we had make us want to go back to those places. The feeling of eating until we were satisfied, and every bite being a gastronomical jubilee, calls us inlanders to return someday for a repeat of the same. Until then, store-bought fish provide a poor substitute to what we had on Vancouver Island and at the Florida coast.

Such was the culinary plight of some sojourning foreigners who had left Egypt with the Israelites. In Numbers 11:5, the unhappy travelers were grumbling about the food. Knowing how vivid the memory of tasty fish can be, any fisher can understand how tempting it must have been to want to go back to Egypt when they were feeling so dissatisfied. But how unwise it was to complain "in the hearing of the LORD" (verse 1). The result was that the anger of the Lord "was kindled, and the fire of the LORD burned among them and consumed some of the outskirts of their camp." The people then cried out and Moses prayed until the fires went out.

Hungry and hard to please, the people wept and said, "Who will give us meat to eat?"

With that attitude they looked longingly backward at the fish and other foods of Egypt. The odd thing was, they were free from the bondage that had tortured them there. And, because they were following God, they were being fed with the miracle food from heaven. Yet, they still complained! What a sad commentary on the ungrateful hearts of the people. It is strange that they could be witnessing firsthand the supernatural deliverance and provision of the Almighty God and at the same time be so wishful for their former lives. How foolish!

There was a time when all of us who are followers of Christ made the conscious decision to walk away from the "pleasures of Egypt." Gladly, we began to seek God, fixing our eyes on pleasing our righteous Father in heaven. But, as is the usual case, the enemy of our souls looks for our weaknesses and entices us with the things of the world that once tantalized our fleshly appetites. How many of us have whispered to ourselves in the deepest recesses of our hearts, "I remember the fish I ate in _____." With that, sometimes our gazes turn back to former pleasures that called our names…and we respond.

Is that very thing happening in your heart? If so, resist the call to return to "the world" for its supply of artificial happiness. Instead, keep walking with God and He will satisfy your longings. God supplies the "miracle food" of the joy of following Him—and no banquet will ever compare to the manna of knowing Christ!

Thank You, Father, that You brought me out of the bondage of the world. I confess there are things "back there" that tempt me even now. I remember how they tasted and felt. Do help me resist them and continue on this journey with You without complaining. In Jesus' name, amen.

27

Big Bang Breakfast

In the beginning God created the heavens and the earth.

GENESIS 1:1

When I shook the hand of a friend at church one Sunday morning, I apologized because my fingers held the residual odor of smoked salmon. I told her I had received a shipment from some folks in North Pole, Alaska, and had enjoyed a portion for breakfast. She smiled and made me promise I would treat her to the tasty fish someday in the future.

Triggered by the mention of breakfast, I asked her to tell me about something I'd heard that had happened in her home a few weeks earlier. It involved a morning feast she had prepared for a guest.

Though he was a friend, the visitor did not embrace my friend's Christianity, especially her stance on the biblical account of creation. His belief was in the theory that at some moment in ancient history there was a sudden explosion of matter, and the result was the formation of the universe as we know it.

Our friend suspected that her guest would continue in his acceptance of the "big bang" hypothesis for at least two reasons. One, it was, in his mind, a viable explanation for the unknown. Second, and more likely, to accept the truth that God was responsible for creation would mean he would have to admit the Almighty existed and that he would inevitably someday face Him for judgment.

Searching for a way to convince her nonbelieving visitor, she decided to try something unusual. When early morning came, she prepared a wonderful, southern-style breakfast. It included all the trimmings presented on a beautiful setting of her best china dishes. The aroma of fresh coffee, bacon, eggs, and biscuits filled the house. When her guest appeared in the dining room, he inquired, "Did you do this for me?"

His question opened the very door she'd hoped for. Without hesitation she answered, "Actually, it was early this morning that I heard a big explosion in the kitchen. Surely you heard it. I came running into my dining room and, lo and behold, this breakfast was sitting on the table! I'm not sure how it happened, but let's enjoy it!"

The man took the bait just as she planned. "Of course, I don't believe you, and I know what point you are trying to make," he said. Then, as if divinely planted in her head, my friend gave her skeptical guest a challenge when she asked, "How could you possibly believe in something so extreme as the big bang theory of creation if you can't believe in my 'big bang' breakfast?" With that, he grinned and recognized her victory.

I have a feeling that every time he sits down to eat his breakfast these days, he remembers my friend's probing question. It could very well chip away at his unbelief until one day he'll accept the truth! I'm glad I already embrace it—how about you?

Father in heaven, I agree that You alone created the heavens and the earth. You are in charge of it, and in that truth I rest. In Jesus' name, amen.

28

Who Built the Boat?

Whatever your hand finds to do, do it with all your might.

ECCLESIASTES 9:10

Those who go down to the sea in ships, who do business on great waters, they have seen the works of the LORD, and His wonders in the deep" (Psalm 107:23-24). In Bible times, long before airplanes were available to carry land lovers from shore to shore, the boats that sailed the great waters of the planet held a place of prominence in the hearts of travelers. In these crafts, some of the most memorable events took place with our blessed Savior. From His famous instructions to the fishermen to cast their nets on the other side where they found a huge catch to waking from His sleep below deck and calming a raging storm, Jesus' presence on the water seems frequent.

One day, while reading one of the stories of Christ at sea, a thought occurred to me. In order for this divine account to have been given, there had to be a ship. "Who built it?" Except for Noah, the shipbuilders' names are never mentioned. Only their products get the coverage. Though this is true, the quality of their workmanship had to be good enough that, for example, in the midst of a storm a ship would hold together so a divinely ordained miracle could be accomplished.

Somewhere in a dry dock, a craftsman engineered, shaped, and pounded on the carefully chosen wood that would become a boat. As the sweat poured from his brow and blisters boiled on his rough hands, did he ever dream that the outcome of his toil would eventually become part of an account stamped into the pages of Holy Scripture?

The worker was probably doing what he did best and earning a wage so his wife and children could eat. More than likely, the man was only being faithful in the small things.

Today, many of us feel that our "daily grind" is reducing our fates to a pile of useless dust. For some, the mundaneness of our work is the very reason we go fishing—to add variety and joy to our lives. The therapy of a day on the water is good medicine for sore, working hands.

When it is time to go back to the "shipyard," or wherever it is we clock in to make a living, we should keep an important truth in mind: In God's scheme of things, that which we do faithfully may be used by the Lord's hand to do something eternal!

Lord, though You know I am grateful for my work, You also know there are times I dread to go back to it. There are days when it seems that not much is accomplished by it. Please help me remember that my diligence to be faithful to my job and to do the best I can will not go unnoticed by You. If nothing else, the mouths I am able to feed by working this job may someday share Your goodness with others. What a great reward that would be! In Jesus' name, amen.

29

The Garage Studio

Then You will delight in righteous sacrifices.

PSALM 51:19

When Nathan reached a high level of skill with the operation of recording equipment and sound engineering, the need arose for a home studio. The two things required were space and money. Unfortunately, there was only one place for the studio—the garage. And even more of a downer, the item that occupied that area was our best source for the extra money needed to buy the big items needed to set up for recording. It was our 17-foot, combination fish/ski boat.

We wrestled with the decision…and the winner was called "PJ's Recording Studio," named after my dad who did the interior construction for the rooms. It was terribly painful to say goodbye to our sleek, well-powered fiberglass friend. But in order to give Nathan the best tools to produce the recordings necessary for our music careers, the sale of the boat was unavoidable.

While the kids struggled with missing our trips to the lake for skiing and tubing, I dealt with another consequence. My fishing from a watercraft was reduced to a canoe. No longer would I have the luxury of screaming at eye-watering speeds across the lakes on a perfect plane and going quickly to the remote honey holes I had memorized. Instead, I was limited to staying within sight of the put-in ramp. Plus, getting a skier up with a canoe and paddles is really tough!

Several disadvantages of trying to adjust to the 14-foot canoe were revealed. Perhaps the worst was not having a trolling motor so I could guide the craft quietly and carefully into the banks for the good fishing. Without it, the wind had its way with my existence on the lake. Like a red-and-white bobber bouncing on the surface, I was a toy in the hands of any breeze that came along. It was frustrating.

Oh, how I longed for the smell of that outboard engine exhaust and the feel of the throttle stick in my right hand. I was left to only dream about the steering wheel that filled my left hand and jerked only slightly when the lower unit plowed powerfully through the waves. But it was not to be, so I resolved to fish only when the weather was absolutely calm.

The backside of the lake became a distant memory. However, six recording projects later I was convinced we did the right thing. Documented in the digital realm are the results of the sacrifice our family made. While I honestly miss the boat and all the fun we had in it, I have to admit that much was accomplished because of its absence. The exchange was basically one boat for 60 songs that have touched the hearts of a lot of folks. And my son, Nathan, found meaning and purpose with his incredible musical and technical abilities instead of wasting his time in the halls of the malls.

For years, when I pushed the canoe off the grassy banks of nearby lakes, I invariably thought of that motorboat. But in the quiet of the waters where I paddled along, I heard the echo of music coming from the garage studio. It's in those moments that I realized the truth that sacrificing for the sake of the Lord is a good thing.

Father, You sacrificed so much for me—even Your Son, Jesus. Help me be willing to always embrace sacrifices for You and Your work here on this earth. In Jesus' name, amen.

30

So Billy Can Go Fishing!

*And He said to them, "Follow Me,
and I will make you fishers of men."*

MATTHEW 4:19

One of the most inspiring statements I have ever heard came from Ruth Graham, the wife of Dr. Billy Graham. It was reported that she made the comment to a young musician during the 2000 Music City Crusade in Nashville. Apparently, one of the lead members of a guest band that was lending their music to the event went to Mrs. Graham and asked if his group could do anything special for her or her husband. Her response was profound: "Young man, your job is simply to fill up the pond so Billy can go fishing!"

Embodied in her words is a concept every church member should understand. Sunday after Sunday our pastors offer the products of hours, even years, of study and prayer. Poured into their sermons are the emotional blood, sweat, and tears required to offer solid biblical insights that will help guide us. Yet, after all they invest, too many of them only have empty pews to preach to.

Inviting lost souls to our churches so they can hear the gospel message is, of course, not the only way to fish for people. But it is certainly one of the most effective means to accomplish the goal. We shouldn't forsake "one on one" evangelism, but to waste our steepled buildings by allowing them to host only handfuls of souls who are already saved is a shame.

I'll never forget the comment my father often made when we would come home from church on Sunday. Sometimes we would tune in to a football game on TV and see the gigantic stadiums filled with people in the stands. With a tone of exasperation that was a result of having preached his heart out that morning to a half-full room, he would gaze at the huge gathering in the football arena and say, "I have a feeling no one had to go door to door and invite those folks to show up." His sincere desire for some help in bringing hearts to the pews of the church echoed in his words.

Having lived in the home of a pastor and knowing how the hearts of God's workers yearn for their church members to assist them in carrying the load of "bringing in the sheaves," I make this appeal to you: Consider what you can do to help stock the pond so your pastor can go fishing!

Father in heaven, thank You for Your abundant love for me. Help me reach out to those who have not heard Your saving message by inviting them to my home church. And, when they come, bless those of us who will be fishing that day. In Jesus' name, amen.

31

Fun and Flies

He restores my soul.

PSALM 23:3

Humans and frogs have at least two things in common: fun and flies. We say, "Time flies when you're having fun." They say, "Time's fun when you're having flies!" Thankfully, they have been chosen to consume the disgusting insects. For us, unless we are yawning on a fast-moving motorcycle, we are privileged to find joy in using flies. We humans who fish can feed the appetites of our adventurer hearts by throwing out fake flies with lines and leaders and rods.

There's something very satisfying and restful about gently and accurately laying a chosen bait on the surface of a slow-moving pool. That alone is plenty of reward. Add the sudden explosion of water and the exciting pull of the line and you have the necessary ingredients to make the icing that goes on the adrenaline cake.

Stepping down off a bank into the cold, uneven bed of a trout stream and feeling the weight of the water press my rubber waders against my legs is a step of bliss for me. And how often it is needed! Getting away from the phone, fax machines, the Internet, and the busy streets filled with exhaust fumes creates a precious time. Sometimes a fellow just needs it. Occasionally, a person has to put the brakes on and take a breather before he or she breaks! If not, a mind can snap like 10-pound test line being yanked by a 90-pound striped bass!

All fishers will appreciate Psalm 23:2-3. The passage was custom written for them: "He makes me lie down in green pastures [taking a break from fishing and having lunch]; He leads me beside quiet waters [Yes! Back to fishing]. He restores my soul [Caught one!]."

Why is this psalm so important? Here's one reason: Unlike frogs, who know how to sit motionless for long periods of time in order to outsmart a skittish insect, most humans do not naturally embrace the skill of resting. We so easily yield to the temptation of being overactive. The balance between work and rest has been sadly lost.

It is important to take note that a primary word in the definition of "restores" is "rest." We can take a valuable lesson from our little green friends. We would do well to be content, at least every once in a while, with ceasing from our labors. Everyone needs the benefits of taking a break by having fun. May you see the fun in stopping for a while to have…that is, to cast some flies.

Father, I come to You for rest in my soul. Help me do it more often! In Jesus' name, amen.

32

The Fish that Caught a Man

*Yet no sign will be given...but
the sign of Jonah the prophet.*

MATTHEW 12:39

Perhaps the most notable catch in the pages of the Old Testament Scriptures was not of a man hooking a fish, but the fish that caught a man. Most of us know the story of Jonah. In Jonah 1:17, we discover that his disobedience to God's call to cry against the wickedness in Nineveh resulted in him being swallowed by a great fish.

While he was wallowing in the smelly entrails of the fish, Jonah probably had no idea there would come a day far into the future when his name would be honored by Jesus Christ, the Savior of the world. Instead, his concern at the moment had to be that his body, not his name, would tumble across the lips of the huge sea monster that held him captive. Jonah's reward for enduring such an incredibly gross, three-day experience was that he became a sign—a picture—of what the obedient Christ would accomplish through His death, burial, and resurrection. How did that come about?

The sign-driven scribes and Pharisees (see Matthew 12:38) were bent on requiring Jesus to perform a miracle in order to attest His credibility. However, Jesus knew that no matter what He did, their insatiable craving for such confirmations would never be satisfied. So He used such human frailty as Jonah's stubbornness to explain His eventual victory over death! It was as though He were clearly contrasting

Jonah's freedom from his bondage to the legalists' endless enslavement to doubt. The point was their need for a Savior!

Perhaps some of the same doubters who scoffed when Jesus refused to "perform" for them that day had an awakening a short time later. In the moment they heard that the grave had released Jesus after three days, perhaps they suddenly understood His reference to the ancient prophet. From that day on, when Jonah's name crossed their minds, their thoughts probably went to the only true source of liberty—the risen Christ.

For those of us who have received Jesus into our lives, we can claim something in common with Jonah. At one time, because of our disobedience and rejection of the Lord's love, we have seen the ugly insides of the "belly of hopelessness." But blessed is the day when, through the redeeming grace of God, we were released. In that hour we became a sign to others that God is the Deliverer!

Knowing that Jonah's name is now synonymous with the finished work of Jesus, a question arises: Will your name remind people that Jesus is alive and well?

Lord, thank You for delivering Your Son from the jaws of the grave. I rejoice that His life has been passed on to me. Help me in everything I say and do to bring honor to Your good name. Amen.

33

Snagging the Snake

Resist the devil.

JAMES 4:7

I only wanted to see if I could pester the slithery intruder as it wiggled its way past my boat. The snake was about 30 yards off my starboard side and, from my aft perch, I could see it was probably about four feet long. The open-face reel neatly and quietly unraveled the line as my bait flew over the snake and dived into the water. It had landed just inches beyond the critter. When the line settled on the lake it fell right onto the snake's back. It slowed as I began to gently reel in.

I'm not quite sure how I managed to do it but the treble hook on my lure snagged the target and the next thing I knew my rod tip bent sharply down and I had myself a situation. The catch and release method of fishing sure started looking like a good idea. However, try as I would, I could not separate my unwanted guest from my hook.

I decided to reel him in closer to the boat and try using my oar to knock him off the expensive lure which was too valuable to lose. When it was within a few feet of the hull I lifted the slimy thing out of the water and held it out at rod's length. He writhed wildly in protest.

Thinking I might be able to sling the thing off, I decided to attempt a cast. It would save me from having to dig for the oar. As I brought the rod and reel over the boat to get into a casting position, the inevitable happened. The snake fell off my hook and right into the middle of the boat!

Needless to say, I headed for the highest point of my rig, the swivel seat behind me. I had no idea what kind of snake I had inadvertently invited on board but I knew things were getting serious.

As the bewildered creature began to search for cover I went for the oar. Beating it to death was not my preference but I was more than willing to have a change of heart. Then I remembered my hook. I thought, *Why not resnag him and try lifting him out of the boat?*

At this point I was very open to forfeiting my lure and feeling safe again.

So that's what I did. With hopes of not snagging the carpet, I placed the lure over the snake's back and gave it a jerk. Yes! It was hooked. With that accomplished I lifted him out of the boat, dropped him into the water, and quickly cut the line. Somewhere today there is a snake slithering around the lake with a colorful ornament permanently stuck in its side. I hope its friends are impressed!

I learned a big lesson that day. Toying with a serpent is not a wise thing to do. Next time I see one invading my space, I'll just watch it from afar.

The spiritual application in this story is obvious. Taunting the enemy of my soul is asking, almost daring, him to come aboard my vessel. Starting the engine and leaving the area is the smart thing to do!

Lord, I admit I am often tempted to toy with things that are unholy—to entertain their presence. Forgive me for being so foolish. Help me keep my spiritual hook and line in the safe places and resist the enticements of the devil. In Jesus' name, amen.

34

Special Delivery

Let your father and mother be glad,
and let her rejoice who gave birth to you.

PROVERBS 23:25

As my parents' fifty-third anniversary was nearing, I began the challenging process of trying to buy them the right gift. I knew finding something they didn't have was next to impossible. All their years of practice at accumulating and eliminating had helped them finally reach that place of rest that is only found between having and wanting. They are living proof that contented people are very hard to buy for when it comes to gifts to honor them on special occasions. I felt a growing turmoil in my gut as each day passed and my wrapping paper was yet unused.

Finally, I thought of the perfect present—me! I was excited when the idea came. "I'll show up unannounced and surprise them with a visit," I said to myself as I ran to the calendar to check my travel schedule. When I saw I had a two-day window to make the 400-mile trip (one way) to West Virginia from Tennessee, I made my plans to go.

A few days prior to my departure I called home. My mother answered. "Mom," I started, "are you going to be home Tuesday afternoon?"

"Yes."

Exactly what I wanted to hear! "I have a delivery for you that evening, and you'll need to be there when it comes. It's an anniversary gift."

"We'll be here, son. We'll make sure we're here."

With that, I waited for Tuesday to arrive and headed for West Virginia. I can't tell you how thrilling it was to cross over the bridge into my hometown knowing my folks had no idea I was so close. Rarely does anyone pull the wool over their eyes. Their intuition has been so well refined through the years that they can smell a surprise a mile away. But not that day. It was one of a very few times they were taken completely off guard.

I love to mentally replay the moment when I knocked on the door and said hello to the more than half-century sweethearts. Mom was visibly short of breath with shock. She threw her arms out and we hugged. Dad couldn't believe I had gone to so much effort just to wish them a happy anniversary. I felt good from my head to my toes. I had done the right thing.

As they told me how they had spent their day sitting in shifts in the living room, waiting for a delivery truck to pull up to the house, I enjoyed the report of their expectations. Any type of recognition for their special day would have made them happy, but, they assured me, I was far better than a bunch of flowers or a basket of fruit.

The visit was all too brief, and I embarked on the journey back to Tennessee. As I watched their house disappear in my rearview mirror, I thought of the commandment that I had managed to fulfill for a day: "Honor your father and your mother, that your days may be prolonged in the land which the LORD your God gives you" (Exodus 20:12). I was grateful for the time to visit them, the resources for the trip, and most of all for the desire to go see them.

Lord, I know there are many ways to honor my parents without being present in their lives. Living for You is certainly the best. Help me show my love by making the effort to visit them as often as I can. Please bless them and keep them in Your care. Amen.

35

The Dragnet

The kingdom of heaven is like a dragnet cast into the sea,
and gathering fish of every kind.

MATTHEW 13:47

The closest thing I've ever done that resembles using a dragnet is seining for minnows in our local creek as a young kid. Two wooden tomato stakes, some twine, and a yard of cloth from one of my mother's bolts of dress material, and I had myself a device I could use to gather some good fishing bait.

I can recall rolling up my pants and sleeves and stepping into the muddy floor of the stream. As the silt clouded the water I would begin to corral whatever life existed beneath the surface. Being careful to keep the cloth against the bottom of the creek bed I would excitedly direct my catch to a corner, then pick up the seine and head to the bank.

There in the middle of the dirty, dripping cloth were a few little, flopping minnows, perfect for my fishhook. Along with the usables would often be a disgruntled crawdad or two or maybe a baby sucker fish. They would get tossed back into the creek. The chosen few would be carefully handled and dropped gingerly into a bucket of clean water.

Little did I know those many years ago that I was recreating a picture of the kingdom of heaven. Found in Matthew 13, the dragnet is cast into the sea and gathers all kinds of fish. Then the catch is brought on shore and sorted, with the "bad" being thrown away.

In verses 49 and 50, the picture is carried even further and, to be honest, it's a sobering analogy. Unlike my choice as a youngster to put the unusable critters back into their watery homes, the hosts of heaven will not be so accommodating: "So it will be at the end of the age; the angels will come forth and take out the wicked from among the righteous, and will throw them into the furnace of fire; in that place there will be weeping and gnashing of teeth."

There is no way to avoid the divine dragnet that is going to be used. Our only hope is to be among the fish placed in God's container of grace. By accepting Christ, the only Son of God, and leaning on Him to cleanse us from our sins, we can escape being cast into the fiery furnace! Now that, my friend, is truly good news.

Knowing what lies ahead for all who swim in the waters of time, it is no wonder that Christians are called to be "fishers of men." After all, swimming next to us in our workplaces, schools, neighborhoods, and even in our homes are fish doomed to be cast away. Compassion cries out for us to tell them about the impending harvest. Through Christ, everyone can be saved if they'll only accept His invitation!

Oh, God, how grateful I am that You redeemed me and prepared me for the dragnet. Because of Your Son and His finished work on the cross, I have hope that I will not be thrown away when You do Your divine gathering. Thank You for Your amazing grace. Help me tell those around me about Your great love for us all. You are the only hope of salvation. In Jesus' name, amen.

36

"It Is I"

*When the disciples saw Him walking
on the sea, they were terrified.*

MATTHEW 14:26

There have been windless mornings when, instead of immediately disturbing the surface of an unusually calm body of water with the splash of a falling lure, I chose to spend a moment admiring the water's glasslike state. Sometimes it looks as though I could literally step off the bank and walk on the water to the other side. It has even crossed my mind a time or two to give it a try, but I hate getting my clothes wet on chilly mornings.

As difficult as it is to imagine anyone strolling across the surface of the water, I accept the report that Jesus did. Believing He was capable of defying the laws of nature in such a way requires a certain level of childlike faith, but if I am willing to embrace the truth that He rose from the dead, I'm not going to doubt He could step confidently onto the seas. This incredible miracle bolsters an even greater truth, especially when it is understood that His walk was on treacherous, stormy waves. That He walked on the water is amazing enough, but even more spectacular was the *timing* of the miracle.

The account in Matthew 14 reveals that it was in the fourth watch of the night—just before dawn—that a contrary wind was causing the seas to batter the disciples' boat. As the frightened and exhausted men fought for survival, they looked out across the water and saw what appeared to be a ghost. The fear that gripped them was strong enough to cause the burly fishermen to cry out.

Jesus didn't let their terror linger. The passage points out that He immediately spoke to them. How compassionate of Him to quickly comfort their troubled hearts. What He said to these fear-weakened sailors was all they needed to know they would be safe: "Take courage, it is I; do not be afraid" (verse 27).

Imagine the elation that must have replaced the disciples' despair. In one moment they were helplessly crying out; in the very next they were filled with confidence that all was well. What made the difference? Was it that Christ came walking on the water? No. The sight of Him heightened their fear because they thought He was a ghost. Instead, it was not until He spoke the words "It Is I" that the storm in their souls subsided.

Jesus doesn't want us to focus on what He can do; instead, we are to be comforted by the fact that He is always present. You and I did not witness the divine event that night that took place on those treacherous seas, yet the precious words the disciples heard echo through time: "It is I; do not be afraid." May they bring comfort to your heart when you're being tossed by a raging storm.

Jesus, I cling to Your words to Your disciples when they were fearful on the raging seas. I know I'll need them when the storms come into my life. Thank You for the comfort of knowing You are always near. Amen.

37

Dumped On!

*Blessed are you when people insult you and
persecute you, and falsely say all kinds of
evil against you because of Me.*

MATTHEW 5:11

My daughter, Heidi, and I joined our friend Randy in Gulfport, Mississippi, for a two-day fishing trip in the Gulf of Mexico. We motored 45 miles out to fish deep. What happened not many minutes after we arrived will never be forgotten.

When we reached the first oil rig that towered high above the water, we stopped beneath it and prepared our gear. Having been at the rig on a previous trip, we knew it usually hosted large schools of red snapper and we were excited to bring in a few. As we positioned the boat to fish, Heidi announced, "Hey, Mr. Randy, there's someone on the rig today!" Although it was occupied, our host assured us that whoever Heidi had seen would not mind our presence. However, we didn't know what mischief loomed above us.

As we put leaders on our lines we stood on the open deck of Randy's nice, beautifully restored 1969 Seabird. Suddenly, I felt raindrops. I thought it odd that the clear skies would be yielding rain. Then it occurred to me that it must be condensation drops from the AC unit on the rig. However, in the next moment the droplets turned a brilliant blue color. I looked up just in time to see the skies above us let go. The three of us scrambled for cover as the raw, unfiltered sewage mercilessly splattered on us and the sickening, pungent aroma invaded our nostrils.

Instantly we knew the man on the rig had dumped his entire septic tank into Randy's boat, right on top of the three "intruders" aboard.

The lumpy liquid that fell on our heads and shoulders was indeed some of the grossest, foulest smelling stuff we have ever encountered. We gagged and gasped for fresh air as we leaned over the railing of the Seabird for relief. We began flailing our arms to rid our skin of the debris and Randy quickly grabbed the spray hose to clean us off. The problem was that the source of water from which the pump was drawing came from around the boat. Basically, he was repeating what had just happened because the area around us was polluted. We were, to say the least, in a real mess.

As the terrible realization gripped us that we had literally been "dumped on," all of us began to moan. It was absolutely one of the most unpleasant experiences of our lives.

"How could that fellow have done such a thing?" we asked each other. "And why?" To this day we are puzzled that anyone would do a deed so despicable. We also wonder if his crime against our humanity was deliberate. Though we probably should've given him the benefit of the doubt, we couldn't help but agree that he knew we were there and that his motives were less than honorable. We were innocent, yet the potty persecution was dropped on us. Everyone who hears our tale agrees that we were sorely wronged and that the story really stinks.

Matthew 5:11 has a familiar ring to it in light of what happened to us in the Gulf of Mexico. But verse 12 adds, "Rejoice and be glad, for your reward in heaven is great; for in the same way they persecuted the prophets who were before you." Far worse than what Heidi, Randy, and I had to deal with, there are people who are "dumped on" because of their stand for Christ. Many have endured torture, persecution, and even murder for the sake of righteousness. These folks are indeed the blessed ones. In the United States, most of us who face the ire of the wicked find it happening at our jobs, in classrooms, in public office, and in other places where slander can be thrown at believers in Christ. While bodily harm may not be an issue, the suffering of the heart is very real.

Have you been "dumped on"? While you endure the foul odor of insults, let it comfort you that you are numbered among "the prophets who were before you."

God, help me in the hours when persecution is falling on me. You alone can cause me to rejoice in those dreary times. In Jesus' name, amen.

38

Light Tackle

*God has chosen the weak things of the world to
shame the things which are strong.*

1 Corinthians 1:27

Sometimes it's not the size of the fish that counts but how light the tackle that was used. I've heard folks in our area boast just as proudly about a 20-pound catfish caught with 6-pound test line as I've heard professionals brag about 400-pound billfish taken in the deep seas with their standard equipment. It simply takes a great deal of skillful finesse to get a fish to the net with undersized gear.

One of my favorite rigs to use is my tiny, open-face reel and its companion rod that is spaghetti noodle thin at the tip. Fighting a hand-sized, Tennessee bluegill with it feels like I'm wrestling a small whale. What fun! And it's extra rewarding when I let youngsters use it so they can experience its sensitivity. Nothing works better for hooking a kid on the joys of fishing than lightweight tackle.

One of the world records for this fishing phenomena is reported to have taken place in California waters. The angler battled a 133-pound yellow tuna for more than 18 hours using 20-pound test line. It absolutely baffles the brain to think this amazing feat was accomplished. It has to be one of the wonders of the world of fishing. How can something so weak outlast something so strong? The answer is found in the hands of the one handling the rod and reel.

A fisher's interest in defying the odds by using the weak to defeat the strong bears a striking resemblance to a trait of our Father in heaven.

He is not reluctant to do the same. In His hands, David overcame Goliath. Gideon and his 300 men were like a weapon in the Lord's hands that He used to defeat vast armies. And without question, the grandest of them all was His only Son, Jesus. Through Christ an eternal victory over death, hell, and the grave was accomplished. Why does God operate this way so often? First Corinthians 1:29,31 reveals the answer: "So that no man may boast before God...That, just as it is written, 'Let him who boasts, boast in the Lord.'"

Glory never goes to the tackle when the report comes that a great fish has been landed with it. Instead, it goes to the one who used his or her know-how to bring the fish to the net. The same is true for those of us whom God uses to accomplish a good deed. May we remain silent, like a rod and reel, so the world around us will give God the glory!

Father, thank You for using me. Though I am weak, I know I can be mighty in Your hands. And may the glory go to You, and You alone, if anything is accomplished. In Jesus' name, amen.

39

Little Bells

And its tinkling may be heard when he enters
and leaves the holy place before the LORD.

EXODUS 28:35

Wwhen I was much younger, the little bells that hung around the necks of stuffed toys and were found on the strings of baby's shoes had great value to those of us who enjoyed night fishing. As a matter of confession, we were known to "rip them off" and tie them to the tips of our rods. Then, whenever a fish was taking our bait, the bells would jingle in the dark and we would excitedly jump to our feet and run to set the hook. The fun we had on the banks of the Ohio was immeasurable. A good fight between an adult catfish and a teenage kid makes for the best of times.

The sound of the bells had a way of making a long wait worth every minute. If we talked at all around the campfire, we kept it to a whisper. We didn't want to miss the tinkling signal. Our ears were carefully tuned to the tips of our rods. Things may be more advanced nowadays in terms of the warning systems for night fishers, but we were proud of our ingenuity.

Bells have been used through the ages as audible indicators that something is happening. Doorbells, church bells, sleigh bells, trains, lighthouses, and dinner bells are just a few. One of the more interesting ways bells were used is found in Exodus 28:33-35. It is written that in the hem of the priestly garments Aaron wore were sewn bells of gold between blue, purple, and scarlet pomegranates (representations of the tree). The purpose was extremely important. "It shall be on Aaron when he ministers...so that he may not die" (verse 35).

One scholar points out that the people who served in the area of the holy place had their ears finely tuned to the bells. As long as they heard their gentle dinging, they knew Aaron was moving around and completing the procedures required for pleasing God. Thus, they knew their safety and atonement were ensured. If the sound of the bells suddenly stopped, fear probably gripped their hearts in dread of the possibility that their priest had died. The consequences would have been devastating physically and spiritually.

Thankfully, believers today don't have to deal with this worry. Christ became our high priest, and His sacrifice at the cross, once and for all, atoned for our sins (see Hebrews 2:17; 4:14; 7:24-28). As a result, bells on the hems of garments are no longer needed. No one has to be anxious that our Savior might die. He has done that already, and now He lives! May the sound of the tinkling bells on our rods bring us happiness. And because of Christ's finished work, may the eternal silence of priestly bells bring us joy and comfort.

Thank You, Jesus, for taking away the worry that the bells will stop ringing. Thank You that I can rest my heart in Your provision of salvation. Amen.

40

The Ripple Effect

...visiting the iniquity of fathers on
the children and on the grandchildren
to the third and fourth generations.

EXODUS 34:7

Imagine a small farm pond. It's early morning and there is a pictur-esque mist framing the water. The surface of the pond is absolutely motionless, as smooth as polished stone. Its color is taken from the sky above and from the trees that line its banks. The air is still.

Now, in your imagination, pick up a rock about the size of a golf ball. Stand at the edge of the water and toss the stone high into the air out over the pond. Hear the ker-plunk as the rock falls into the liquid and is swallowed by the splash. Watch and wait.

Can you see what's happening? Radiating out all around the spot where the water was suddenly troubled are ripples. These round evidences of agitation cannot be turned back no matter what you do.

This is what happens when a person makes a decision. In the moment a course of action is taken, whether verbally, physically, or spiritually, it sets in motion a ripple effect that sometimes is good and sometimes not so good.

A prime example of how one person's choice affects many others is the tragedy of someone deciding to climb behind the wheel of a car while intoxicated. In the Fort Worth, Texas, area in 1998, a man who was severely impaired by drinking alcohol plowed into a car that contained four beautiful high school girls. The innocent young ladies were killed. All the parents and siblings were completely devastated by the drunk driver's choice. But the trauma was not limited to the immediate families of the girls.

The citizens of the town, the county, and the region were divided by the court case. Because it was the man's first offense, some people thought he should get a seriously reduced punishment. On the other hand, some folks were convinced the driver should be given the death sentence. No one came through as a winner in this case. And for decades to come, the ripple effect of the drunk driver's shameful decision will be felt. The sobering truth that the choice of one person will eventually touch the life of another is clearly supported in Exodus 20:5-6: "You shall not worship them [idols] or serve them; for I, the LORD your God, am a jealous God, visiting the iniquity of the fathers on the children, on the third and the fourth generations of those who hate Me, but showing lovingkindness to thousands, to those who love Me and keep My commandments."

In light of the truth in this passage, we need to be willing to look beyond ourselves and see the future effects of our current decisions. As we resist the longing for the self-satisfaction found in the unholy pleasures of the moment and, instead, choose righteousness, the ripple effect of obedience will go on through the years.

Father, I know my choices will eventually wash over many souls in this life and in the generations that follow. I need Your grace and strength to be a blessing to them. In Jesus' name, amen.

41

Top Angler

Can you draw out Leviathan with a fishhook?

JOB 41:1

Unless I am misunderstanding the tone of God's questions to Job that begin in the thirty-eighth chapter of that book, it is my perception that God had already done all the things He was asking Job if he could do. And if the trail of His awesome abilities is followed, an important discovery is made for anglers everywhere. Beginning with Job 38:12, consider these great feats:

> "Have you ever in your life commanded the morning, and caused the dawn to know its place?" (verse 12).

> "Have you entered into the springs of the sea?" (verse 16).

> "Have you understood the expanse of the earth?" (verse 18).

> "Have you entered the storehouses of the snow, or have you seen the storehouses of the hail?" (verse 22).

> "Can you lead forth a constellation in its season...?" (verse 32).

> "Can you send forth lightnings that they may go...?" (verse 35).

> "Do you give the horse his might?" (Job 39:19).

> "Is it by your understanding that the hawk soars...?" (39:26).

"Is it at your command that the eagle mounts up and makes
his nest on high?" (39:27).

This abbreviated path of God's unending capabilities leads us to
the first verse of chapter 41. It is here that a fisherman's ears will perk
up: "Can you draw out Leviathan with a fishhook?" The fact that God
includes the world of fishing in His discourse to Job should encourage
any angler who might presently be in despair.

While very few of us can say that the depth of our valley would
compare to the canyon that Job walked through, still our need to be
uplifted is very real. For both Job and us, the God who comforts our
hearts is the same. His amazing strength, evident in the way He man-
ages His awesome creation, brings us renewed hope in His ability to
sustain us. After all, if He can land leviathan, He can surely get us to
the safety of His net!

*God, I am humbled by the realization that there is nothing I can
do to rise above Your awesome skills. It is an honor to be called
Your child. In Jesus' name, amen.*

42

White Bread Wisdom

Cast your bread on the surface of the waters,
for you will find it after many days.

ECCLESIASTES 11:1

I t would be hard to number the times I have sat on a bank or in a boat with rod in one hand and a sandwich in the other. Lunch rarely interrupted my fishing, nor did fishing interrupt my lunch. I love to eat while angling. One day my daughter quipped, "What if we were like fish and suddenly a hamburger dropped in front of our faces and dangled there. Not able to resist it, we would grab it and start eating. Suddenly, without warning, we would be rocketed skyward. Then we'd know how those crappie feel!"

One particular thing I have done many times as a fisherman involves having food around water. Whenever I do this thing I always remember a specific Scripture in the Old Testament. My favorite sandwich to enjoy while fishing is peanut butter and strawberry jam on white bread. It takes longer to eat it than any other type because of the gooey peanut butter.

Without fail, there is always a little part of the bread that didn't get a covering of the spread. That's the part I usually reserve for the resident minnows and small bluegill that can't resist coming to the top and snatching it. I am intrigued by their willingness to risk fins and scale to have some bread.

What is particularly interesting is when the white bread hits the water it immediately begins to distribute itself into a thousand little crumbs. I'm not sure what it is about white bread that makes it happen, but the floury cloud spreads quickly and the little fish seem eager to begin battling for the pieces.

The sight of the scattering crumbs reminds me of today's verse. To this day I wonder what the bottom-line meaning of that verse is. There are commentaries that give good insights, and I have come to accept at least two of the possibilities. One suggests that it refers to liberal, charitable giving without expecting an immediate realization of gain. This notion makes great sense when linked with Luke 16:9: "And I say to you, make friends for yourselves by means of the wealth of unrighteousness, so that when it fails, they will receive you into the eternal dwellings."

The other view of the "bread upon the water" passage is that it is wise to make prudent investments in several ventures, not limiting business to a single trade. In other words, don't put all your eggs in one basket. The New English Bible translates Ecclesiastes 11:1-2 in this way: "Send your grain across the seas, and in time you will get a return. Divide your merchandise among seven ventures, eight maybe, since you do not know what disasters may occur on earth."

Both of these interpretations are appealing. One is for the person who possesses an unusually hearty gift of giving, and the other is for those who have the talent to do business. Following the advice of either of these offers great returns on investments.

The benefit I may get for feeding the little fish my white bread may be that they are made a little larger because of the meal they consumed. In turn, I may catch them later when they're big enough to qualify for a spot in my skillet!

Father, thank You for Your infinite wisdom that is found in everything You have made. Help me cast Your bread onto the waters for Your glory. In Jesus' name, amen.

43

If I Could Be a Fish

Whosoever loses his life for my sake...

LUKE 9:24

If given the opportunity to be any fish that ever swam the waters of the earth, I know without a doubt which one I would like to have been. Though it might seem the obvious choice, it would not have been "Leviathan," the name often used to describe a great whale or sea monster. As enticing as it would be to take up such a large space in the ocean, I would pass. Nor would my choice be the great fish that was used to teach Jonah a lesson. Throwing up is not one of my favorite things to do.

The one and only fish I would like to have been is mentioned in Luke 24:36-43:

> While they were telling these things [the news about seeing the risen Christ], He Himself stood in their midst. But they were startled and frightened and thought that they were seeing a spirit. And He said to them, "Why are you troubled, and why do doubts arise in your hearts? See My hands and My feet, that it is I Myself; touch Me and see, for a spirit does not have flesh and bones as you see I have." And when He had said this, He showed them His hands and His feet. While they still could not believe it because of their joy and amazement, He said to them, "Have you anything here to eat?" They gave Him a piece of broiled fish; and He took it and ate it before them.

To have been the fish that was caught, prepared, and used as proof that Jesus was alive again following His crucifixion and burial would undoubtedly be a high honor! Of all the fish in the seas, that one gave its life for the moment when the resurrected Christ used something natural for the purpose of giving credibility to something supernatural. His eating, a normal human pleasure, served in showing the doubtful and frightened people that the one who stood before them was God in the flesh. To have been part of that incredible manifestation would be a joy beyond measure.

The good news is that I can still be like that fish. Though the biblical account of it is past and sits with immeasurable importance in the history of our Savior, the opportunity is still available to be used as proof that Jesus is alive. Believing that I have been caught by the Holy Spirit of God and I am being made more like God each day by His work in my heart, I consider myself "consumed" by Christ. As He takes me in, a doubtful world watches. Like the men in the Scriptures who thought Jesus was a ghost, many people today are afraid and doubtful of Him. Yet it is in His willingness to accept me, embrace me, and use my life that they can know He is real.

With that as my hope, that fish and I have something in common. We are both in Christ! Blessed be His name.

Jesus, please continue to use me to show a lost, dying, and hopeless world that You are alive. Make me worthy to be consumed by You. In Your name I ask this, amen.

44

The Hook

The passing pleasures of sin...
HEBREWS 11:25

Why does it happen that the injury which sends us to the emergency room so often hurts only half as bad as what they do to us when we get there? I'll never forget the treble hook I accidentally buried into my thumb. Because it happened instantly, the pain I felt the moment it went in was surprisingly minimal. I immediately tried backing it out but due to the barbs it wouldn't move. It tore at the inner flesh. That hurt!

After several minutes the pain had increased to a point that I knew I had to get some help. My friend Tommy Villers suggested pushing it on through and snipping off the barb but I couldn't bear the thought of it. Instead, I let him carefully snip the hook off at the lure and I headed for the hospital with it dangling from my thumb. What a mistake! I should have followed my friend's advice. But what did I do? I voluntarily hurried to the emergency room for some real torture.

By the time I reached the doctor's office, the area around the imbedded metal had grown very tender and sensitive. However, that pain was mild compared to what I felt when the doctor put the needle tip next to the hook and...*s l o w l y*...pressed it in. It was unbelievable. I was a teenager at the time, and today, 35 years later, the scream I let go still echoes in the valley near Fairmont, West Virginia.

I suppose the doctor believed that he and four others would have had to hold me down if he tried pushing the point of the hook through the meat of my thumb without numbing it first. But what did he know? I honestly think it would have been easier without the Novocain. I hope I never get another chance to find out!

The pain of the hook injury was not in the going in. It was in the coming out. What a vivid picture this is of what happens when we allow sin inside and it gets its barbs into us. The entry doesn't hurt. In fact, there is a certain pleasure, though passing, that accompanies the taking in of sin. However, when it begins to fester and turns nasty in the soul and body, it is not so easily removed.

A drug addict, for example, will testify to this truth. Initially, putting drugs into the body has its highs. After a while, however, the physical and mental toll it takes becomes too much to handle and eventually the time comes for detox. Without eliminating the source of pain, death is inevitable. As pleasurable as sin is at first is how painful it is in the end.

Of course, not all sins we inflict in our lives are as overtly harmful as drug use. It doesn't take too long to see the changes in an addict's body and demeanor. Other sins are slower to kill. Pornography, for example, might not be as drastic in its quickness to deteriorate a healthy body, but the damage is inevitable and undeniable. There comes a day when a man (or woman) realizes the ruining effects of pornography are visible in his marriage, his family, and even his work. Hiding the constant feeding of an insatiable and escalating appetite for sensuality, the growing disrespect for women, the loss of hard-earned money, and, in some cases, the contracting of a deadly disease are a few of the symptoms of doom. Sadly, he wakes up one day to find his life is in shambles. It didn't start that way, but that's the way sin always ends.

To remove the imbedded spiritual and emotional infection caused by months and years of indulgence in immorality can be excruciating. Why? For one reason, the person must go through the incredible pain of humbling himself and asking for help. Second, he must begin fighting the war against the desires of his flesh. That daily battle alone will be the most agonizing part of the healing. Once the "barb" is cut, deliverance will come. Only the Great Physician—Christ alone—can perform that surgery effectively.

The smart thing for me to have done that morning so many years ago was to more carefully respect the presence of the hook. So it is with sin. I know it's all around me. To avoid it and show a sober regard for its potential for harm is wise. And remembering that sin hurts far worse coming out than going in is a powerful motivator to righteousness.

Lord, how grateful I am that You removed the hook of sin when You died on the cross for me. Help me handle my life with great care and avoid letting unholiness snag me. In Your name I pray, amen.

45

Stewards of Terror

The fear of you and the terror of you
will be on every beast.

GENESIS 9:2

Fishing and hunting have been longtime winners on our home's list of enjoyable things to do, at least for me and my two children, Nathan and Heidi. Annie has never taken to the idea of sitting for hours on a deerstand or handling wiggly nightcrawlers with her bare hands. The kids and I understand her reluctance to venture too far outdoors past her flower garden, but we appreciate her willingness to embrace our adventures.

As it turned out, there was a convenient division of interests that developed among our children when it came to the water and woods. Heidi took to fishing with a passion that would rival Simon Peter and his brother Andrew. Nathan, on the other hand, was our Nimrod. In the middle was a papa who desperately loves to do both. I could not have taken a state-of-the-art computer and engineered a better situation for myself. To have two kids whose affections were so evenly disbursed allowed me to span the entire year in the pleasure of entertaining the joy they each found in the outdoors. What a blessing!

Of all the elements of each activity I wanted to teach them, perhaps one of the most important had to do with attitude more than aptitude. While showing them skills such as casting and shooting was a great deal of fun for me, there was something to be learned that was of greater import. I wanted them to deeply respect the *life* of the creatures we would capture and consume. To go to a deerstand or a lake without regard for the blood that flowed through the veins of an animal or a fish was not allowed. There had to be an understanding that while we as humans have dominion over all that flies, crawls, or swims, these creatures do have feelings. According to today's Scripture, their root emotions in regard to the presence of humans is fear and terror.

I managed to teach Nathan and Heidi that shedding the blood of the game had to be accompanied by a certain remorse. Without it, we would merely be murderers. I realize there seems to be a great conflict between these two ideas. But believing that mankind has a biblical right—and even a duty—to "harvest" the fish, animals, and birds for food means we are not restricted from the pursuit. While we admittedly enjoy the challenge of developing and using the skills required to outsmart our prey, we cannot come to the moment of taking their lives with a casual spirit.

Many nights following a kill earlier in the day, I have laid my head on my pillow and been unable to fall quickly to sleep. I know it sounds odd, but I am invariably haunted by the sight of a creature that has died at my hands. I can only hope that my children will carry this strange irony of the heart through their hunting years.

I watched their faces closely after they took their first deer and caught their first fish. I was determined that if they didn't show that hint of hurt for what they had done, I would find a way to divert them from taking game. Fortunately, they both accepted the knowledge that they are the carriers of terror into the minds of the creatures they hunt and fish. With that, they have been added to the number of good and conscientious sportsmen and sportswomen.

Today, Heidi and her husband Emmitt, and Nathan and his wife, Stephanie, will have plenty of opportunities to pass the attitude of respect for life on to their children.

O heavenly Father, keep me mindful of the value of life and cause me to be a wise steward of the terror I bring to the creatures I pursue. In Jesus' name, amen.

46

Caught at the Pond

For My eyes are on their ways...nor is their
iniquity concealed from My eyes.

JEREMIAH 16:17

I can't stand it any longer. I have to try. I know no one will see me do it under the cover of darkness." I was mumbling these words to myself the night I gave in and walked through the darkness to fish in the pond behind the house where we lived years ago. When we first looked at the place to consider buying it, I noticed the small lake that graced the community. It was fenced off, and I learned from the real estate agent that it was for a good reason. The folks who owned it did not want young children playing around the water because of the legal ramifications of an accident or even a drowning. The scuttlebutt from the neighbors was that the pond owners were vigilant about guarding their property and that absolutely no trespassing was allowed. Because of that report, I never asked to fish in the pond, assuming the answer would be a firm *no*.

In the two years I had lived at this location, I didn't see one soul drop a line into the pond. It pained me that due to such tight security around it, a grand opportunity for fishing was being unnecessarily squandered. The ache to find out what size bass or catfish might have been there for the catching grew worse every time I mowed the yard, raked the leaves, washed the car, or played with the kids in the back of the house. It tortured me to look at it. Then one evening as the sun was setting, an idea came to me as I sipped a cup of coffee on our deck and listened to the gurgling spring pouring into the far end of the one acre lake.

Waiting until the night sky was completely black and the area around the pond was dark as coal, I quietly gathered my rod and reel and headed to the backyard. With the stealth of a fox, I found my way to the fence at the edge of the pond. The only thing that separated me from the edge of the water was about six feet of nicely mowed grass. I knew all I had to do after casting the lure was to be careful not to tangle up in the chain link fence.

The two-inch strip of raw bacon from our refrigerator that hung on my hook lightly splashed when it fell into the deep end of the pool. I let it sink a little and then tightened the line. With one eye on the house above the opposite bank I held the rod in my hand and waited for a strike. I would like to tell you that something immediately hit my hook and nearly ripped the rod out of my hands. I wish I could say that my suspicions that the pond was filled to the brim with trophy fish begging to be caught were proven true. But nothing happened.

In the actionless three or four minutes that I waited for a bite, something inside me began to grow more and more uncomfortable. I felt like I was being watched. I checked all around me but saw no movement and heard no stirring. While I was sure I was fishing unseen, there was a gnawing awareness that I was already caught. And then it hit me.

I had gotten so involved in the attempt to test the lake with my bait that one important truth was ignored. I realized I was feeling guilty because the Lord was watching. Surprise! Guess who was caught at the pond!

Without delay I reeled my line to the bank and gave it an upward jerk. Rats! I was hung up in something I couldn't see. *Serves me right*, I thought. I wrestled with the snag for a few seconds and breathed a sigh of relief when it let go. With the tail of my ego tucked under me I headed back to the garage and put my gear away.

To this day I don't know if there were sizable fish in that pond. I never did go back to it. But I did go to the Lord and ask Him to forgive me.

Father, help me always remember that no matter what I am doing or where I am going, Your loving eyes are following me. To know You are watching moves me to righteousness. In Jesus' name, amen.

That Smile

An excellent wife, who can find?

PROVERBS 31:10

I will be forever grateful for the incredible technology of recording events. Because it exists, I was able to see something I would never have otherwise seen (unless, of course, God has His divine recording equipment on constantly and lets us all watch later on).

As impossible as it seemed, my firstborn was now married. It was a beautiful ceremony that lasted a brief 33 minutes and happened in a blur. It seemed to go by as quickly as the previous 20 years. Suddenly "little Miss Heidi" was Mrs. Emmitt Beall.

I didn't faint as we walked the aisle together. We talked the whole way. She said things like "slow down." I'm not sure if she was implying "Are you anxious to get rid of me?" or "Let's make the most of this stroll!" I like the latter idea better.

When the preacher asked, "Who gives this woman away in marriage?" I nearly answered, "My mother and I do." I had practiced my one line over and over and kept thinking about what not to say. I almost messed up. After I lifted Heidi's veil and kissed her cheek, I turned to Emmitt and said, "You're getting the only little girl in my heart!" and then I took my place in the pew next to Annie. The two of them turned to face the altar and that was the last I saw of their faces until they were pronounced man and wife. I had no idea what I was missing—but then I saw the video.

Our friends, Joseph and Dana, graciously agreed to record the ceremony, and they were thorough enough to conceal a camera up front near the choir loft. It faced the bride and groom. The angle was perfect to film Emmitt and Heidi's faces as they repeated their vows, took communion, and exchanged rings.

To say that the video is valuable is a gross understatement. I wouldn't take the proverbial farm in Georgia for it. Had the camera not been rolling, we would have missed some of the most telling expressions on two young faces anyone could imagine.

Of all the looks we were able to capture, unseen to the audience, there is one moment that I will cherish forever. It was that instant when Emmitt responded to the vows with his answer "I do." As the lines were fed for him to repeat, I could tell Heidi was listening very closely. I knew she was because she usually tilts her head sideways when she is at full attention. As she is hearing Emmitt's flawless delivery of the spoken vows, Heidi's face suddenly had a look that seemed to ask, "Will he say he will? Or will he back out of this?" Her expression turned slightly worried.

Then the preacher got to the part when he asked Emmitt to respond with "I do." At that point Heidi was looking at the floor. Oh! The apprehension she felt. It was obvious. However, in the very next instant, everything changed. When those two words came confidently across Emmitt's lips, Heidi suddenly looked up and smiled ear to ear. I could tell her quiet fears had turned to an undeniable joy.

As Annie and I sat on the couch the night after the wedding and came to that special moment of the film, I couldn't help but add my commentary. I rewound the tape and paused it at the very point Heidi looked up and smiled. "Annie," I said as I leaned forward, "I've seen that expression before. I know what she's thinking. I saw that smile in the Gulf of Mexico when she caught the 51-pound cobia. I saw it when she felt the 30-pound flounder take her bait off the coast of Canada. That look is unmistakable." I then said the words out loud as the image froze on our screen: *The hook is set!* I knew Emmitt was caught, and he wasn't gonna get away. (Of course, he didn't want to!)

I've watched that video several times, and I have to rewind it over and over to see that happy expression. One thing is for sure, behind it is a young lady whose character is as excellent as her beauty. Our son-in-law will enjoy his years of learning that Proverbs 18:22 is absolutely true: "He who finds a wife finds a good thing and obtains favor from the LORD."

Someday I want to take the two of them fishing in deep waters so Emmitt can see "that smile" in its original form. It will warm his heart just as it does mine!

God, bless my children and their spouses as they walk together through the years. Give them cause to smile because of Your sweet presence in their lives. In Jesus' name, amen.

48

Fish the Opposite Way

"I'm going fishing."

JOHN 21:3

I can only imagine what it was like on the shore of the Sea of Tiberias among the group of men that had gathered there. Simon Peter, Thomas, Nathaniel, the sons of Zebedee, and two other disciples were biding their time. Who knows what they might have been doing. Skipping rocks maybe? That's what Charlie, Ken, Jim, and I did when we stood on the shores of the Brazos River in Texas many years ago during a camping trip. It's normal to compete that way when water is close!

On the shore of Tiberias, Peter apparently couldn't bear the inactivity so he suddenly announced, "I'm going fishing!" It seemed like a good idea to the others so they said, "We'll join you." That night they fished and fished. However, not one fin touched their nets. Why they fished all night is puzzling. They weren't returning to fishing as a career. The fishermen among them had long forsaken their permanent work on the boats. But the heart of a true fisher loves to catch, not just cast. They must have gotten into the challenge a little more seriously than they planned. The next thing they knew, daybreak had arrived.

Suddenly, from the shore, a stranger asked, "Children, you do not have any fish, do you?" That's one question any fisher hates to answer in the negative. However, they ate the humble pie and answered, "No."

Then came the well-known command, "Cast the net on the right-hand side of the boat and you will find a catch." They followed the instructions and the haul was beyond their imagination. It was then they realized the stranger was Jesus. Peter had been through the scenario before, and he surely had no doubt who he was seeing (see Luke 5:1-11).

Much could be gleaned from the scene that took place that morning with Jesus and the humble fishermen. Perhaps one of the most inspiring points to ponder about it is that it wasn't until the Lord got involved and suggested they go the opposite way with their nets that anything was accomplished. This is a truth played out over and over in the Scriptures, and I've seen the same thing in my life as well.

When Annie and I first started "fishing" in the music business, we kept dropping our lines in one specific place, hoping for a response. We plodded along for three years with hardly any results. Then one day in the back room of our home church, as I sat monitoring the TV screen and assisting in the recording of the service, the call from heaven's shores came quietly to my heart. "See those faces in the audience? There are families sitting out there in desperate need of encouragement. You think you know many of them well. However, beneath their well-dressed surfaces are hearts that are troubled and breaking. Go encourage the families."

My heart nearly broke when I realized what the Holy Spirit was whispering to my mind that Sunday morning. I went into that little sound room fishing on the left side of the boat. I came out with a resolve to cast our net on the opposite side.

As a result, Annie and I became oddballs in the Christian music business. With a lyrical focus completely centered around family, we were hard to sell to a broad music market. But we kept fishing. That was more than 35 years ago, and we're still at it! Nearly 30 recorded projects, over two dozen books, and a travel schedule that keeps us busy clearly represents God's goodness in filling our nets.

Perhaps you are hearing the call to cast your net on the other side. It seems scary and totally wrong, but if you know it is the Lord calling from the shore, do what He says! If you choose His way, check your nets. They'll need to be strong!

Thank You, Jesus, for Your wise guidance. Help me listen for Your instructions. Blessed be Your name. Amen.

49

Little Is Much

*There is a lad here who has five barley loaves
and two fish, but what are these for so many people?*

JOHN 6:9

The story of the little boy with the five loaves and two fish that Jesus used to feed the 5000 is recorded in all four Gospels of the New Testament. Its extensive coverage indicates that important lessons exist in the account that should not be ignored. One of the most valuable is that little is a lot with God!

The youngster who followed the crowd to the mountain to hear Jesus teach had much more food than one kid could eat. Why so many loaves and fish? One notion I find reasonable is that he intended to make a little money for his family by selling his goods to the crowd. (Instead of a lemonade stand, he was going to have a fish sandwich booth.)

Perhaps out of curiosity, the boy must have moved within close proximity of the Lord. The young fellow suddenly found himself facing a business decision that didn't fit the norm. If the conjecture regarding his motives are correct, this must have crossed his youthful mind: "If I give this stuff away, I won't make a cent. I'll go home with empty hands and an empty cash box. My folks won't like it!" But as everyone knows, he gave his all for the sake of Christ. In His hands, the sustenance was blessed, broken, and bountifully distributed to fill the needs of the hungry. Therein is one of the great lessons of the story. One small offering, compared to the size of the crowd, resulted in one huge return.

I've often wondered what happened to the 12 baskets of loaves and fish that were left. Who eventually got the bulging baskets was not included in the story. Why would Jesus allow such an overage? I like to believe the excess went to the young man. Within a relatively short amount of time, the boy went from a small fish sandwich stand to the beginnings of a chain of restaurants! How delighted he must have been to arrive home with his haul. Can you imagine the surprise the parents must have felt when the helpers started dragging in the loaded baskets? Not only was there an abundance of food for the family, but plenty to sell in the streets. And it all happened because one small boy gave everything, as little as it was, to the Master. That's one kid every person would do well to look up to!

Father, how gracious You are to take our small offerings and create such large results. Each time You do, it is an encouragement to give again. I know the very best gift I can give You is my life. I want to put it into Your hands because I know You can make the most of it. I do pray, however, for the strength and grace to endure the breaking as You multiply my worth. In Jesus' name, amen.

50

Don't Hoard the Hog

Freely you received, freely give.

MATTHEW 10:8

After a summer day's work on the construction of a new 14-acre lake at the farm of our friend Joe Goodman, he asked me to stop by his house. He announced that he had a gift for Annie and me. When he pulled the package out of his refrigerator and put it in my hands, the weight of it was surprising.

"What's this?" I inquired.

"That's home-processed bacon. I slaughtered it, butchered it, salted and preserved it just like my daddy did it years and years ago."

Joe was proud of his offering to us, and he had full right to be. He had skillfully prepared the hog in the old-fashioned way. I opened the package and sniffed the large cut. The aroma sent my mind flying like a rocket back to Godby Branch in West Virginia, where I had smelled that kind of bacon in my grandma's house.

Not only was the meat good when sliced and fried with eggs and biscuits (watch out for the drool!), it also added a dandy taste to cooked beans of the pinto and green variety. A hot pan of cornbread, a bowl of bacon-flavored beans, an onion, and a cup of coffee is the meal that is served to real champions. I am happy to say that I have personally tasted that culinary glory!

When I arrived home with the pork prize, Annie put her smeller to the slab just as I had done. Her eyes went heavenward as she took in the memory of years gone by. We immediately cut a portion and tossed it into the skillet. Within minutes we were wiping grease off our chins that were tight with grins that stretched ear to ear. Forget the health of the heart for the moment, let the taste buds rejoice.

We were due to drive to West Virginia a few days later and as we made our plans to go, I suddenly got an idea. Assuming it had been a long time since my mother and father had enjoyed a helping of the kind of bacon we had in our possession, I cleaned out a cooler and put some ice in it. When I handed it to my folks, their expressions were absolutely priceless as they inhaled the familiar aroma. They groaned in joy at the thought of reconnecting to a taste that had been too long missed. We stood in the kitchen of their home and admired the evidence of "the way they used to do it."

A huge smile swept across Dad's face when I told him I was going to leave the heavy slab with them. I assured them Joe wouldn't mind. With the bacon nearly clutched to his chest, he had that look on his face that said, "Go get the green beans and let's start snapping!"

What transpired in the next moment is something that will be forever etched in our memories as one of the funniest ever in our family. Dad immediately started talking about how to cut and freeze the oversized chunk of meat. Fearing it might be far too long before just the two of them could consume the entire thing, Mom challenged Dad's plans to "hoard the hog."

"PJ, we can't eat all of that meat. We'll have to share it with some friends."

Without batting an eye, he looked around at everyone, slightly bowed his head, and said with an Academy Award-winning tone of manufactured pity, "But Lillian, we have no friends."

We nearly split a gut at Dad's profoundly quick wit. His way of saying, "Ain't nobody gettin' one ounce of this bacon" was a worthy candidate for the Chapman humor hall of fame.

Later reports from my mother revealed that Dad had given in. He enjoyed the taste of the past so much that he couldn't help but call in a few old buddies and let them savor a walk back into their own childhoods. The bacon was a big hit with everyone who was privileged to partake.

Joe shared his hog with me; I in turn shared it with my folks; and they imparted the bliss of the bacon to their friends. Such is the joy of generosity.

Thank You, Father, for Your generosity to me. May I never be guilty of being stingy with all You have given me. In Jesus' matchless name, amen.

51

Casting

Cast your burden upon the LORD.

PSALM 55:22

One of my favorite parts of the fishing routine is casting. There is something in my psyche that allows me to feel very satisfied when I see my bait splash a mere inch or two from where I wanted it to fall. To know my eye/hand coordination is working well is most rewarding. If all I got done at the lake was a good day of accurate casting, I could go home with no reason to complain. Hooking a fish, of course, takes the joy to the next level, but I refuse to complain if it doesn't happen.

Engaging in the challenging activity of trying to toss bait at a certain spot reminds me of biblical casting—casting our anxiety on Jesus and casting our burden on the Lord (see Psalm 55:22; 1 Peter 5:7). How privileged we are as God's people to be able to share our worries with our loving, heavenly Father. I shudder to think of what despair we would experience if He were not willing to receive them.

There is one major difference between casting as a fisherman and doing it as a burdened child of God. When we cast our fishing lure, it is still tethered to us by the line. That means we fully intend to retrieve it. In essence, we never plan to let go of it. Even if we find a snag, we are reluctant to give up trying to free the lure.

In 1 Peter 5:7, however, the word "casting" implies a simple action as opposed to a continuous action: "casting all your anxiety on Him." It's a one-time thing. This is where the difference lies. Our burdens must be cast completely away. Throwing our cares in God's direction must be done with no plans to pull them back.

What is the reward for sending our concerns to the Lord? We can rest assured that we get something incredible in return. It is revealed in the second part of Psalm 55:22: "and He will sustain you." What greater catch could anyone expect?

The next time you are standing on a bank or sitting in a boat fishing, let the motion of casting remind you of the grand opportunity afforded God's people. Then throw your cares on the Lord!

Jesus, thank You that I can cast my cares on You. There is no one else in this universe who loves me that much. Amen.

52

No Court Jesting!

Let your speech always be with grace.

COLOSSIANS 4:6

I don't mean to be disrespectful with my question, but have you ever contemplated what it might have been like to sit around a campfire with the group of fishermen called by Christ to be His disciples? I can't help but wonder if their conversation was typical to what usually can happen when men get together. I find it amazing how quickly our conversations can turn from redeemable to rank. It seems there is something in testosterone that goes wacky when too much of it is concentrated in one room. Within mere minutes a group of guys can swing from subjects as worthy as social issues to talk of how an untimely escape of flatulence brought the house down at church. What on earth is it about us that so easily gives way to this kind of behavior? (Women certainly want to know!)

Engaging in "men talk" is, I will admit, one of the most pleasurable things I can think of. I have had more good medicinal dosages of laughter when among men than nearly any other setting. The challenge is to keep the conversation to a careful degree of decency. While it should be a battle fought by every man, it is not so easy to win.

The task of striving to keep clean talk is best learned at an early age. However, there is a problem for many dads who want to teach their kids to avoid foolishness. It is that too many of us men are just grown-up boys. We have our own mouths to watch, and that alone is a monumental assignment. To add the responsibility of helping someone else guard their speech puts real tension on the brain. Consequently, the toughest place to teach this lesson, for me at least, was in the classroom of my home.

When our children were much younger, I started feeding them the following passage found in Ephesians 5:4: "There must be no filthiness and silly talk, or coarse jesting, which are not fitting, but rather giving of thanks." I tried to get the point across to the kids that Paul was not trying to be a party-pooper in addressing the matter. Instead, he was providing a wise guideline of holiness for the saints of God to follow. One high goal of maintaining purity in speech, I told them, was found in Ephesians 4:29: "Let no unwholesome word proceed from your mouth, but only such a word as is good for edification according to the need of the moment, so that it will give grace to those who hear."

Of course, Annie and I were to be good examples of walking the talk. In order to keep the above passage at the forefront of all our minds, I lifted the phrase "no coarse jesting" from the Scriptures. Whenever I sensed their verbiage (or behavior) was getting out of hand, I used the quip like a whip to correct them. Naturally, they managed to rewrite their own version of the phrase. Their motto became, "No *court* jesting!" I heard it said that way each time I parentally interrupted their sessions of questionable conversation. (Even Annie would yield to a streak of mischief from time to time and repeat the altered phrase. The kids loved it.)

Their humorous response didn't surprise me, nor did I always correct it—even when they danced like jesters as they said it. I would chuckle with them and rest in believing the message was getting through. Eventually, the kids began to monitor their own behavior. The instant one would recognize wayward conduct coming from the other the reprimand would be delivered: "No court jesting!" And they were even careful to help dad out with his occasional struggle for sanctification. More than once when they heard or saw me stray, one of them would remind me with the altered version. I was grateful for the help!

I have a feeling that someday in the future, if little ones come along that look (and act) like their Grandpa Chapman, they too will be introduced to this important behavioral concept and the unique, gentle rebuke.

Dear Lord, thank You for Your patience with me as I strive to walk and talk worthy of Your good name. I commit even now to be careful with every word that proceeds from my mouth. In Jesus' name, amen.

53

Prime the Pump

*Devote yourselves to prayer, keeping
alert in it with an attitude of thanksgiving.*

COLOSSIANS 4:2

Consider these two phone calls. First is two men:

Ring. Answer.
"Hello."
"Hey, Dave, Bill."
"Yeah."
"Wanna go fishin'?"
"Sure. When?"
"Meet you at 6 AM at the ramp."
"Good enough. See ya then."
"Bye."
Clunk

Phone call number two between two women:

Ring. Answer.
"Hello."
"Hi, Trish, Allison here. How are you doing?"
"Oh! Fine, and you?"
"Wonderful. How is Billy doing today?"
"He's much better. He'll probably go to school tomorrow."

And off they go on a dialogue that lasts nearly 15 minutes. Finally, these words come…

"Trish, the reason I'm calling is to…"

I'm not sure why men are usually not as quick to engage in in-depth conversation as women. There is one theory I lean toward: Men would rather "do and talk" than just talk. This is accurate as far as I'm concerned. The two men in the phone call will get to some wordier times when the lures start flying. That seems to be our nature. The two women, on the other hand, seem to enjoy conversation without the distraction of action. Most ladies I know don't need an activity to help them communicate.

Men seem to thrive on motion during conversation. It's as if the movement of their arms or legs keeps their lips pumping. In general, whenever the action stops, their mouths likely stop as well. Fortunately, it doesn't take a tremendous amount of motion to work the jaw of a fellow. Someone once said that the closest thing to nothing a man can do and still be doing something is slowly reeling in a lure. It gets as close to fulfilling the call to "be still" as anything else. Besides, the ever-so-small circles of a turning hand can generate enough power to pull thoughts from deep within the soul of an angler. It's amazing how much information can be brought to the surface when even the smallest, lightweight reel is being operated.

This is why praying and fishing go so well together! Talking to God is undeniably the most important conversation a person can ever have. And since movement seems to be the best trigger for communicating, what better thing could a fellow do than fish and pray? For example, with such minimum action required to monitor a bobber bouncing in a pond, pouring our hearts out to the Lord while doing so can be accomplished with an effectiveness that can be life-altering.

I know there are innumerable things guys can do to siphon words out of their hearts. But if you find yourself doing something alone, like fishing solo, may you use it as an opportunity to talk with your Savior. It's a great way to prime the pump!

Lord, thank You for wanting to hear from me. I pray for Your great assistance in being a better communicator with You. You know my heart, and You know I enjoy "doing" while I'm talking. Please hear my cries and keep me moving closer to You. In Jesus' name, amen.

54

The Float Plane Fib (Almost)

Therefore, laying aside falsehood,
speak truth each one of you with his neighbor,
for we are members of one another.

EPHESIANS 4:25

Where the notion came from that fishers have a reputation for stretching the truth is a mystery to me. Wherever it originated, I don't appreciate the accusation because it makes it really tough to convince people that my 22-pound Tennessee bluegill is for real!

Warping the facts in order to conceal the truth is a temptation not limited to anglers. The opportunity comes to everyone at one time or another to alter the accuracy of an account. But when we take the bait of deceitfulness and the hook is set, too many times it results in other people getting hurt.

It was the fear that injury would come to her family that my wife chose the path of righteousness when her chance came to tell an untruth (a nice way of saying "a lie"). Bless her heart. She was forced into the unwelcomed temptation by her husband and kids, yet she maintained a high level of integrity even though it wasn't easy.

It happened in Alaska. I'll never forget it. Our children and I begged Annie to accompany the three of us on a float plane/king salmon fishing adventure. Having much rather stayed in the hotel and read a book, she reluctantly showed up with us at the dock early one morning before daylight.

As the four of us and a stranger sat tightly squeezed into the plane, the pilot was outside checking his equipment. Then we heard him yell at the young dock worker who was preparing the craft for flight. "Hey, did you pump the floats? They're sitting awfully low in the water."

"Yes, sir," the teenager responded.

The pilot grumbled and grabbed a clipboard. I knew what was coming and dreaded hearing the question that had to be asked. I was painfully aware of the offense that was about to be rendered to a woman who didn't want to even be onboard, much less get quizzed about something she never spoke of publicly.

He stuck his head into the cabin and unmercifully asked, "How much does everyone weigh?" As if targeted by fate, he looked at my dear wife and said, "We'll start with you, ma'am."

Time slowed down to a deathly crawl. As if using the pitch control knob on a tape deck and slowing the words to a guttural-type drawl, the words echoed in my head. It was an awful moment.

I dared not look at Annie for fear of getting the same look she gave me during the transition stage of labor in childbirth. It would have been that "I love you but don't ever come near me again" expression.

Annie said she seriously considered lying about her weight but in light of the aeronautical safety purpose of telling the truth, she told the pilot what he needed to hear. She said later that what motivated her most to be honest was seeing, in her mind's eye, the headlines that might have been at the top of the Anchorage daily paper the next morning: "Woman lies about weight, killing entire family!"

We had a great trip into the back country outside of Anchorage. Obviously, we survived the flight, thanks to Annie's willingness to treat the truth with utmost respect.

This true story illustrates one of the enormously important reasons for following the admonition in Colossians 3:9: "Do not lie to one another." It really can be a matter of life and death—physically, emotionally, and spiritually.

Father in heaven, thank You for forgiving me for those times I have failed Your people by altering the truth. Worse, I have failed You. Help me lay aside the old ways of lying and embrace telling the truth without exception. I need Your grace and strength to do this. In Jesus' name, amen.

55

Tom's Shark

For each one will bear his own load.

GALATIANS 6:5

It is odd to me that within a span of only four verses in Galatians 6 today's verse appears preceded by "bear one another's burdens, and thereby fulfill the law of Christ" (verse 2). These thoughts seem to be contradictory. Yet, on close examination of the original language, there is a separation of instruction that not only makes sense but is also sobering in its reality.

Galatians 6:2 centers around gently restoring someone caught in sin. Romans 14:1 and 15:1 encourage the stronger ones among us to accept and bear the weaknesses of those who are immature in their walk with Christ: "Now accept the one who is weak in faith…We who are strong ought to bear the weaknesses of those without strength."

However, in Galatians 6:5, the word for "load" in the original language is *phortion*, meaning to "bear the burden of the consequence for iniquity." Each of us will be left alone to shoulder the millstone—the sin and punishment—that is the result of our actions.

Perhaps a good way to illustrate the truth embodied in the text is through the following story. Mike stood next to Tom at the aft of the boat as he watched his friend crank the reel to the point of exhaustion. The six-foot blacktip shark had no intention of allowing itself to become fillets for someone's frying pan. Realizing his friend was growing more weary by the moment, Mike tapped Tom on his sore shoulder and offered to help. Waiting for the right moment, Tom transferred the heavy rod to his friend. He was grateful for the assistance. After battling the heavy fish for quite a while, it was finally gaffed and placed securely in the huge cooler at their feet.

When the tired buddies looked at their watches, they realized they had to hurry to the dock so Mike could meet a very important business obligation that evening. After quickly trailering the boat and bidding their goodbyes, Mike drove away. In the rush to get to his meeting, he regretfully had to leave Tom with the time-consuming task of cleaning the kill.

While the victory of the catch could be considered *theirs*, not Tom's, the responsibility for the kill unfortunately became his alone. After all, he was the one who hooked it. Though Mike would have gladly helped had he been able to, Tom had to bear the consequence of the catch. So it will be when our time comes to stand before the Lord. Others might help when we're weak in faith, but there will be no other person to face the burdens of our sins. Oh! How precious is God's grace to forgive us!

Merciful Father, I pray for the strength today to live holy before You and to make wise decisions in regard to the temptations that encourage me to sin. Help me keep in mind that if I ignore the work of Christ at the cross, I alone will bear the burden for my transgressions. And, as You empower me to walk with You, I pray for the grace needed to help the weak in faith as we journey along the way. In Jesus' name, amen.

56

Curtain Fishing

*The Spirit Himself testifies with our spirit
that we are children of God.*

ROMANS 8:16

As a kid growing up in West Virginia, one of the highlights of the
year was the annual church fund-raiser fair. The room was
filled with tables and booths that featured crafts, homemade pies, and
other items. All the goodies were designed to capture the cash in the
purses and wallets of those who filed through. It was always a successful event.

It was at the fair that I was introduced to an emotion that I still
enjoy to this day—so much so that I make time and financial sacrifices to experience it. It happened at the fishing booth. It was a corner
area simply equipped and usually manned by two individuals. Sepa-
rating them from the crowd was a tall curtain made from a few bed-
sheets hung over a strand of clothesline that stretched from one wall to
another. The divider that was created spanned approximately ten feet
in width and seven feet in height.

The "fish" the children would catch was a brown paper bag that was
attached to the twine by a hook made out of a clothespin. In the sack
was a plastic trinket. For me, this was not the real prize. As it turned out,
the trophy I landed that first time I went "curtain fishing" is mounted
on the wall of my heart. It was the excitement of feeling the tug on the
pole when the person hidden behind the cloth would give the line a
couple of quick jerks to let me know it was time to reel in my catch.

The tug didn't happen immediately after I cast the twine over the drapery. Because the person behind it had to take a moment to attach the bag to the hook, there was a delay that allowed enough time to let some tension build in my mind. The anticipation was sweet. I could hardly hold still.

Suddenly it happened! I'll never forget the feeling the first time that bamboo pole danced in my hands. There was something mysterious about being connected to the unseen. To know that evidence of its existence had presented itself, and that I would soon be able to see it, was more excitement than a little boy should have been allowed to experience. My heart pounded with joy as if I had hooked a blue marlin off the coast of Florida!

Today, whenever I go fishing, the one thing I look forward to the most is that telltale tug on the line. Without exception, the sensation of an impending catch drives me to the brink of emotional ecstasy. If that feeling wanes, what would be the point of fishing?

Through the years I have discovered a comparison between the jerk of my monofilament and another special "pulling" that takes place in my spirit. That supernatural tug on my heart when God gets my attention either through His written Word or a quiet whisper in my spirit is a joy beyond anything else I can ever imagine. To know that He, unseen with my eyes of flesh, has connected with me in my heart, keeps me going back to Him in the same way the tug on my fishing line keeps me returning to the water.

One of the most vivid recollections of this wonderful interaction between the Lord and me took place the year I first moved to Nashville. I was an unmarried young man pursuing the music business, but it wasn't pursuing me. Frustrated and wondering what to do, I wrestled with whether or not to leave. At the time, I was also a Christian. My desire to follow Christ in obedience in regard to my music outweighed all other hopes. One night as I prayed for guidance, I heard a whisper deep in my spirit: "Put the guitar away." At first I thought the devil himself had spoken. It seemed illogical to cast aside the one gift I could give to the Lord. Then I realized that *God wants me to offer my talent as a sacrifice to Him.* So I literally put the guitar—and all the music and dreams it represented—back in its case and, believe it or not, joyfully said goodbye to singing and hello to submission. Having heard the Lord speak, then obeying, was a much greater satisfaction than making music.

Several weeks later, the reversal of guidance came softly to my heart. "Pick up the guitar again." Once more, I thought evil had spoken. I surmised, *Surely this is not God.* However, I came to realize that He had honored my sacrifice by returning the music to me. With a new attitude I obeyed. Nearly 30 years later, I'm still "pickin' and grinnin' " for Him. What a blessing to have heard His voice. It will always be a welcome tug on my line!

Lord, help me keep fishing for Your voice. Keep me sensitive to Your presence. I will cherish each time You pull on the strings of my heart. In Jesus' name, amen.

The Silver Bridge

You do not know which day your Lord is coming...
For this reason you also must be ready.

MATTHEW 24:42,44

In 1960, my parents moved to Point Pleasant, a beautiful town located on the West Virginia side of the Ohio River. On the southern side of the town, the Kanawha River poured into the Ohio, providing a great deal of fishing opportunity to the locals. Mostly catfish and an occasional carp could be enticed to our bait. The catfish were welcomed additions to our stringers, but the stinky carp usually met their doom and were not allowed to return to the water. (Someone once said, "If you took all the carp in the world and laid them end to end, you should leave them that way." They were right!)

In the heat of summer, one of the best places to fish was in the shade of the great Silver Bridge that crossed the Ohio River on the west side of town. Built around 1924, the well-known link between West Virginia and Ohio experienced a steady growth of traffic as the industry of the region grew. The expanding population resulted in its nonstop use. It became one of our most valued passages as citizens of the two states blended work and family.

Countless times my dad drove the narrow lanes of the bridge with my sister and me in the backseat and my mother up front. We didn't think much about crossing the river on the tall edifice made of metal and concrete. Our minds never once considered the possibility of danger. For all of us who utilized the bridge with such regularity, there was little, if any, thought ever given to the possibility of the disaster that finally struck on December 15, 1967. The following lyric describes that fateful day.

The Silver Bridge

She was built strong and tall 'cross the great Ohio River
I'll not forget the name they would give her
She was known for her color and what she would give
To the town that would call her The Silver Bridge

She was work for our fathers and a nest for the sparrows
And a way to get to loved ones on her lanes that were narrow
And we welcomed all the travelers who were just passing
        through
And we welcomed all the commerce and the good it would do

How many times did I cross that span
That testified well to the genius of man
She was part of our families, a friend to us all
But we never thought she would fall
We never thought that at all

'Cause year after year she gained our trust
And the bright silver paint covered her rust
But the runaway barges, the cold and the heat
Pounded hard on her metal, till she grew weak

Then one evening in December she was full end to end
And her load was just too great with our family and friends
Then she creaked and she groaned, then turned upside down
And her fall filled the valley with a terrible sound

How many times did I cross that span
That testified once to the genius of man
She was part of our families, a friend to us all
But we never thought she would fall
We never thought that at all.

Now if bridges were able I believe she'd have cried
No one come near me, please stay on your side
But now there's forty-four souls resting up on the ridge
And two are still missed with that old Silver Bridge

And now every time I cross any span
I wonder about the genius of man
She was part of our families, a friend to us all
But we never thought she would fall
We never thought that at all.

I was 17 at the time of the disaster. It took a couple of years for the city to repair the sight of the incident and the absence of the bridge on the skyline of town is noticeably missing. But still on the hearts of all who live or lived in Point Pleasant at the time is an emotional scar that will never go away. It binds us together with a common sense of awareness that our lives are fragile. Whenever the memorial is passed when driving down Main Street, the memory of the rumble that shook the city in 1967 rattles our souls. It even affects the way we feel when we cross bridges all these years later. A sobering loss of trust for such expanses resides in our hearts.

There is one thing that haunted me then about those whose lives were sadly claimed on that December evening, and it continues to this day. In one moment they were going about their lives normally, just like my family did when we crossed the bridge. In the next instant, they found themselves crossing an eternal river. In one second they were looking at the car in front of theirs; in the next they stared God in the face.

How utterly fragile our lives are. How incredibly important it is to be ready to make that final crossing.

Father in heaven, make me ready for the hour that will find me facing You. Wherever I am, whatever I'm doing, receive my spirit when it receives the call to cross over to Your side. In the name of the only one who alone can save me—Jesus Christ, amen.

58

Don't Let the Kids Sing

He who rejects Me rejects the One who sent Me.

LUKE 10:16

The huge cobia came lurking near the surface of the boat, and I happened to get a glimpse of it. Quickly I dropped a hook into the water with a tasty cigar minnow attached and hoped the heavy fellow would make another pass. Sure enough he did…and he swam right by my offering of a wonderful meal. Not only once did he reject the minnow, he darted by it a few more times as if to say, "No way, bubba!"

What that fish didn't know was how much he hurt my feelings. When he resisted the bait, he was rejecting me. It was my best effort at choosing a treat for him, and he flashed by it like the hook was empty. How totally rude of him. I felt terribly offended.

This lighthearted look at my less than spectacular moment at sea provides a great picture of what happens when someone is presented with the opportunity to accept the Son of God and chooses instead to swim right by Him. The person doesn't realize that when he ignores Christ, he is also turning away from the heavenly Father.

Apparently, God has feelings that accompany an individual's choice of whether or not he will receive His only begotten Son. Rejection is conducted like electricity from Christ to His Father. Sadness must surely be felt.

An insight that Annie received helped me more fully understand how God must feel when His Son is rejected. It was on a night that she and I arrived at a church for a concert. The first trip we had made to this church included our two teenagers. Nathan had played his guitar and he and Heidi sang. Parentally speaking, their performance was exceptional. They couldn't have done better. Annie and I were obnoxiously proud of them. We were really surprised on our return visit when the directive came to exclude the kids from the stage. Some people in the congregation were apparently unhappy with the youthful style of music our children had presented and would not allow them to sing at their church again.

How close Annie and I came to making an early exit. We were livid. How could they have viewed Nathan and Heidi's music as unacceptable? One acoustic guitar, two voices, and a simple lyric didn't create enough volume to pain the ears of anyone. We were bewildered.

Not willing to breech our agreement, however, Annie and I fulfilled our responsibility with the church and left town. On the way home Annie teared up. I assured her that the kids would be fine and that we would survive the incident.

Her response to my efforts to comfort her was life changing. "Of course, I'm hurt that our children were refused a place in the concert. That didn't feel good. But the truth is, when the staff said, 'Don't let the kids sing,' they were not just rejecting them, they were rejecting me. I think I see, if only a little, how God must feel when people turn away from His Son. It surely must break His heart." The drive back to Nashville was quiet as we pondered the thought.

Now, when I fish for men and someone resists the good news of Christ, I have a better understanding that they are not just ignoring Jesus, they are ultimately rejecting His Father. Sorrow grips my heart because the great loss these people experience is eternal. But even more saddening is the thought of the divine disappointment that must wash over God when His Son is so slighted. It's a pain I never want to cause Him.

Father, I accept Your Son, Jesus. He alone has purchased my redemption. Through Him only can I come to You. Thank You for Christ; I love Your Son. In His name I pray You will receive my adoration. Amen.

59

Miracle Math

Two are better than one.

ECCLESIASTES 4:9

Fishing with a friend has a rare benefit. It is revealed when, for example, the rod suddenly bends downward into the shape of a rainbow and the tip starts dancing up and down. What joy is found in having an audience to view the exciting challenge. Because of someone else's presence the fun of the catch is multiplied. Plus, when the size and weight of it grows with each time the story is told, a friend will smile and vouch for every word!

If, on the other hand, the line snaps and the big one gets away, the grief is not nearly as painful when a caring person is there to sympathize. His or her commiseration is like salve on a wounded ego. Somehow the willingness to keep casting is not as quickly lost when a friend is there to bolster the hope for one more bite.

Fishing buddies are not the only folks who enjoy this shared benefit of friendship. It is also available to those whose lives are meshed together in matrimony. Consider the wisdom heard by my son-in-law, Emmitt, at a wedding. He said it was embodied in the minister's words to the young bride and groom during the ceremony: "Because of your commitment to one another, through the years ahead your joys will be doubled and your sorrows halved."

This beautiful, poetic pronouncement has certainly proven to be accurate for Annie and me. In our more than 35 years of marriage, the joys of delightful events like childbirth (for me, at least), babies' first steps, first home purchased, last payment on a car, and holiday gatherings were twice as nice when shared.

The weight of sorrows, on the other hand, were reduced significantly because we both shouldered the load. We've shared moments that included the loss of a job, the crunched fender (not my doings!), stitches in a child's leg, and bad grades our kids earned. There was also the water-soaked carpet in a flooded basement, the news of a friend's divorce, and, far worse, the passing of a parent. All these events were much more tolerable because we could lean on each other as we walked through them together.

That our joys are doubled and our sorrows halved is nothing less than God's idea of "miracle math." Only someone as brilliant as He could have calculated it. After all, it is only our heavenly Father who can take two human spirits, add them together, and come up with the equation that baffles the greatest of mathematicians: $1 + 1 = 1$. If He is able to manipulate the figures in this way, He is fully able to cause those same two hearts to find great comfort in knowing that together their delights are made brighter and their disappointments made lighter. Blessed be His name!

Thank You, Father, for companions. How gracious of You to create friendships in which Your special kind of calculations can be made. You alone are the author of the miracle math that so profoundly defies the norm. I will forever agree with You that "two are better than one." In Jesus' name, amen.

60

Fishing for Answers

*These words, which I am commanding
you today, shall be on your heart.
You shall teach them diligently to your sons.*

Deuteronomy 6: 6-7

As parents, Annie and I have learned that in order for fishing to happen you don't have to buy a license, get bait, go to a lake with a rod and reel, or own a boat. All you need is an inquisitive child. If you have time to listen, there'll be plenty of fishin'.

One of the first questions I can remember facing came from our only begotten son. He was four years old when we attended a wedding with him. The scene prompted him to seek a rather insightful bit of information. "Mama," Nathan asked as we drove home, "who kept me while you and dad got married?" Not that we had anything to hide, but we were at a loss on how to answer that one. You might say the hook was never set in our brains. We simply diverted him quickly to the nearest fast food, a Happy Meal distraction. We were saved by a burger!

Another interesting question came from Heidi. She was also about four years old when we were traveling through a small Louisiana town. We came to a railroad crossing. The bells sounded and the red lights blinked to warn us a train was coming. I was the first in line when the red-and-white automated metal guards fell across the road. As we sat and watched the train zoom by us just a few feet away, the noise was deafening. Heidi ran to the front of the van and climbed up on my lap.

I could feel she was trembling and seemed seriously worried about something. I assumed the rumbling had frightened her. When the long procession of cars finally passed and the road blocks rose to let the traffic continue, Heidi refused to crawl off my lap and instead grabbed me around the neck with both arms. Not wanting to hold up the drivers behind me, I began to roll forward. When we began to move, her tender chokehold around my neck grew noticeably tighter. That's when she asked, "Dad, when is that train coming back by here?"

I responded with a confident tone. "Sweetheart, it'll be a long while, I suppose. Now get down and let Daddy drive." She seemed to be calm and willingly headed back to her seat.

As the miles went by, I pondered Heidi's question. I wondered what could have driven her to ask it. All of a sudden the reason came to me why she was fishing for the answer to her question. As far as she was concerned, it was a matter of life and death. You see, we had gotten Nathan an electric train set for Christmas just a few weeks earlier. The tracks were assembled in the shape of an oval. Equipped with little houses, cars, and people, and blinking red lights at the crossing, the model railroad seemed quite real to Heidi. As best as she could understand, all trains in the world went in circles. And Nathan's engine and cars were quick to complete the rounds. In Heidi's mind, that train in Louisiana was no different. No wonder she was scared!

The years that followed were filled with inquiries. In the two-and-a-half decades of raising kids, our minds were often the waters where the kids trolled for answers. Sometimes they fished in shallow waters (usually in dad's head). At other times they went deep (that would be in Annie's sea of knowledge). In which pool they dropped a line was never a concern; we were grateful they would come to us when they were angling for insights.

Though there were times they landed little or nothing, Annie and I have been thankful we were there when they needed to catch some answers. Today they are grown and gone from our home, but they know fishing from the banks of our hearts is always in season.

Father in heaven, thank You from the depths of my heart for the opportunity to raise two of the finest anglers who ever lived. Your kindness to help me be a place where my children could hook a few answers is much appreciated. Now I send them to You because, when it comes to wisdom, I know I am a small pond and You are a deep ocean. In You they will find the real trophies of wisdom. In Jesus' name I pray, amen.

If you liked Steve Chapman's
A Look at Life from the Riverbank,
you're sure to enjoy
A Look at Life from a Deer Stand

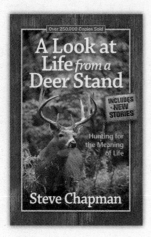

From the incredible rush of bagging "the big one" to standing in awe of God's magnificent creation, Steve Chapman captures the spirit of the hunt in *A Look at Life from a Deer Stand.* In short chapters filled with excitement and humor, he takes you on his successful and not-so-successful forays into the heart of deer country. As you experience the joy of scouting a trophy buck or bringing in a hefty doe, you'll discover how the skills necessary for great hunting can help you draw closer to the Lord.